Contemporary Options
in Eschatology

Contemporary Options in Eschatology

A STUDY OF THE MILLENNIUM

MILLARD J. ERICKSON

BAKER BOOK HOUSE
Grand Rapids, Michigan

Scripture quotations are from the Revised Standard Version unless otherwise noted. The RSV is copyrighted by the Division of Christian Education of the National Council of the Churches of Christ in the United States of America, 1946, 1952, and 1971. Quotations from the New American Standard Bible (NASB) are copyrighted by the Lockman Foundation, 1960, 1962, 1963, 1968, 1971, and 1972.

Printed in the United States of America

To
my wife's parents
Magnus and **Ruth Nepstad**

Contents

Preface

This volume grew out of a request by students at Bethel Theological Seminary for a course that would examine thoroughly and objectively the eschatological options extant in the circles in which they would one day minister. In preparing for that course, I realized that the need for such a study goes beyond the walls of our classroom.

I wish to thank all who have assisted in the production of this work. I am especially indebted to those students who first requested the course and whose questions and comments helped sharpen my thinking. My teaching assistant, Mrs. Ines E. Bowers, read the entire manuscript thoroughly and offered numerous suggestions, particularly regarding stylistic matters. Typing was done by Mrs. Nikki Daniels and Mrs. Aletta Whittaker. All imperfections in the manuscript are of course my responsibility alone.

Introduction

James Orr, lecturing at the end of the nineteenth century, observed that various areas of Christian doctrine had received special attention and development at different periods in the history of the church. Thus in the second century the church dealt especially with apologetics and the fundamental ideas of Christianity; in the third and fourth centuries, with the doctrine of God; in the early fifth century, with man and sin; in the fifth to seventh centuries, with the person of Christ; in the eleventh to sixteenth centuries, with the atonement; and in the sixteenth century, with the application of redemption (justification, etc.). There had been doctrinal convictions, either implicit or explicit, on these subjects previously, but it was as crises arose in these areas at these particular periods that the positions were more precisely articulated.

Orr suggested that the peculiar interest of the modern age is eschatology, the one remaining undeveloped topic of theology:

> Probably I am not mistaken in thinking that, besides the necessary revision of the theological system as a whole, which could not properly be undertaken till the historical development I have sketched had run its course, the modern mind has given itself with special earnestness to eschatological questions, moved thereto, perhaps, by the solemn impression that on it the ends of the world have come, and that some great crisis in the history of human affairs is approaching. Even here I do not anticipate that the great landmarks in Christian doctrine will undergo any serious change.[1]

---

1. *The Progress of Dogma* (London: Hodder and Stoughton, 1901), pp. 29–30.

Orr felt that while the doctrine of eschatology had been discussed in the nineteenth century, it had yet to receive major treatment and the issues had deepened during the last generation or two.

The twentieth century has seen intensive study of several specific doctrines. The first half of the century focused uniquely upon the doctrine of revelation. The doctrine of the church, especially as it related to the ecumenical movement, was discussed at great length in the second quarter, fading gradually in the third quarter. Following that, the doctrine of the person and work of the Holy Spirit received special attention, with the level of concern having now apparently peaked. In more recent years eschatology seems to have moved to the forefront. Movements such as the theology of hope have given eschatology virtually an exclusive domain. In previous times a doctrine required a century or more for thorough delineation, but now, with the acceleration of discussion, research, and communication, the periods may have shortened to a quarter-century or less.

The preoccupation with eschatology has taken different forms in different groups. Within conservative Christian circles it relates to the order of events connected with the second coming of Christ. Conservatives reached a consensus on the major points of eschatology by the beginning of the twentieth century. All human beings (except those still alive when the Lord returns) must undergo physical death, at which time they go to an intermediate state appropriate to their spiritual condition. Those who have trusted themselves to the saving work of Jesus Christ will go to a place of bliss and reward; those who have not, will go to one of punishment and torment. At some future time Christ will return bodily and personally. Then all the dead will be resurrected and consigned to their ultimate destination—heaven or hell. There they will remain eternally in an unalterable condition.

Within this general scheme, however, there has been considerable variation. This has related first to the question of whether there will be a millennium (a thousand-year earthly reign of Jesus Christ), and then, for those who answer yes, to the question of whether Christ will return at the beginning or end of the millennium. Among those who hold that this return will precede the millennium, some believe that the church will go through a time of severe anguish called "the great tribulation"; others that the church will be removed from the world, or "raptured," before the tribulation. Around these issues a considerable amount of debate has taken place in recent years. Whether or not we agree that these are important issues, since those who discuss them consider them important, we must examine them.

The primary purpose of this book is to examine closely these conservative options. In order to place the discussion in a broader context, the first two chapters will examine a number of other alternatives that have been popular in the nineteenth and twentieth centuries. Some of these fall outside the range usually considered evangelical. This will help us understand the general mood or milieu contributing to the construction of contemporary eschatology. Then consideration will be given to the various millennial positions, then to the several tribulational views. As part of this last section, the theological and hermeneutical system known as dispensationalism, which figures so prominently in the tribulational debate, will be closely examined.

The pattern of treatment of each millennial and tribulational position will be the same: a brief overview of the position, its history, a more thorough examination of its major concepts and of the arguments offered in support of them, and finally an evaluation of both its positive and its negative aspects.

The author puts forth this work with the prayer that it will stimulate and encourage the reader's interest in the important issues of eschatology, deepen his confidence in the fact of the Lord's blessed coming, stimulate him to "search the Scriptures" to determine the things which are true, and increase his understanding of and appreciation for the convictions of those whose views differ from his.

Part 1

Background Views

Chapter 1

Schweitzer and Dodd

Introduction

The nineteenth century was in many ways a time of theological turmoil. The orthodox synthesis, while varying from Lutheran to Reformed and even to Roman Catholic, maintained a basic understanding of the nature of theology and had held forth for quite some time. Now, however, new conceptions of the very nature of religion were breaking upon the church, producing more radical transformations of the fundamental nature of theology than had perhaps occurred in all the previous centuries since the time of the New Testament. There had always been radical segments of Christianity, but they had generally been fringe elements. Now these revisions were entering the mainstream of the church.

In large part these alterations resulted from new developments in the world of knowledge which affected traditional doctrines of Christianity. In philosophy the critiques of Immanuel Kant had called into question the possibility of proving the existence of God, or even of having any knowledge of what goes beyond our sense experience. In natural science Charles Darwin's *Origin of Species* challenged the Christian doctrine of the special creation of man. The application of historical and literary criticism to the Bible seemed to undermine some traditional views of the date and authorship of Biblical books, as well as the historicity of large segments of the narratives.

Those who accepted these developments had to find new approaches to theology. For the most part they agreed that the essence of religion in general and of Christianity in particular does not consist of beliefs. One branch fixed religion in value judgments and made Christianity largely a matter of ethics, or what one does. Another, taking the lead of Friedrich Schleiermacher, conceived of Christianity as primarily a matter of feeling. These two branches agreed that Christian dogmas and beliefs must be carefully scrutinized, evaluated, and justified, not simply held credulously. This gave a new cast, or a new key, to theology—including eschatology.

Nineteenth-century Christians, living in the midst of this stormy sea of new developments, were certain of one thing: as Christians, they must in some special way be related to and concerned about Jesus, who was called Christ. This, however, made all the more urgent the question, Who really is this Jesus? The search for the historical Jesus was an attempt to get back to the person of Jesus as He really was. As the searcher for Jesus groped his way back through the haze of centuries of church tradition and theological construction, he would find and describe the life, personality, and teachings of Jesus. He applied to the Gospel narratives the same methods of historical research utilized in investigating any historical events or literary materials.

In theory the searcher was objective, laying aside dogmatic prejudices and church traditions in favor of a more scientific type of research. He adopted the methods utilized by uncommitted historians in the hope of realizing this ideal. His goal was not to defend any particular beliefs about Jesus. If any ideas about Jesus could not be supported by the evidence, so much the worse for those conceptions. Later commentators have questioned whether these scholars were as objective and their method as free from controlling influences as they both claimed and desired.

Applying their research to the Gospel materials, these searchers found an image somewhat different from the conventional one. While the details varied from one scholar to another, the general contour was of a basically human teacher who pointed men to the Father rather than to Himself. Jesus called men to believe *with* Him, not *in* Him.

One of the dominant themes in Jesus' teaching, they said, is the fatherhood of God.[1] God has created all men and continues to give

---

1. Adolf von Harnack, *What Is Christianity?*, pp. 68ff.

life, watching over them as carefully as a shepherd watches his sheep. He knows and protects each of them, just as no sparrow can fall to the earth without the Father's knowledge and permission (Matt. 10:29–31). Jesus spoke of the Father's knowing even the number of hairs on a person's head (Matt. 10:30).

The infinite value of a human soul is a corollary of this tenet.[2] Because God so highly esteems individual men, we also should esteem our fellows. This contributed to the emphasis upon the brotherhood of men. Jesus reduced the whole law to two commands: love the Lord God with your whole heart, and love your neighbor as yourself. If the parable of the prodigal son is the model for the relationship man should have with God, the parable of the good Samaritan is the model for the relationship man should have with other men.

Jesus' teaching regarding the kingdom of God[3] was regarded as basic and central to His entire outlook and message. Albrecht Ritschl, who gave perhaps the most extended treatment of this doctrine, said that Christianity is not a circle, which has one center, but an ellipse, which has two foci—the doctrines of redemption (the operation of divine grace) and of the kingdom of God (the ethical activity of man).[4] This kingdom is an ethical community of men, distinguished by reciprocal action that is motivated by love. The kingdom is established by man but not independently of religious motives. Jesus founded this kingdom. His significance lies primarily in His life, not His death. He is the perfect example of the type of humanity that is to be united in the kingdom. He is the complete revelation of God as love.

While "lives of Jesus" propounded varying ideas of the kingdom, they had one common denominator: God reigns here and now. According to Jesus the kingdom has come in and through Him. It is not an external rule, with discernible dimensions of society as its visible marks, but instead a reign of God within human hearts, a reign that is becoming a reality for an increasing number of persons. Its spread throughout the human race is both

---

2. Ibid., pp. 73ff.

3. Ibid., pp. 56ff.

4. *The Christian Doctrine of Justification and Reconciliation: The Positive Development of the Doctrine*, pp. 30ff.

horizontal (from one individual and group to another), and vertical (from one social class to another).

The kingdom that Jesus brought is different in nature from anything that preceded it. In this sense it had come once and for all. Its nature would not change with passing time. Its growth was one of degree, not kind. As man extended the kingdom to yet more and more areas of society, he would progressively Christianize society. This belief and hope were vividly illustrated in 1908 when a new religious journal was named the *Christian Century*. Behind this name lay the belief that the twentieth century would be *the* Christian century. The kingdom of God was here, or it would be shortly. It would be introduced progressively through the efforts of Christians, not through a cataclysmic event such as the second coming of Christ. The nature of the kingdom now is no different from what it will be at any time in the future. Some who held this view of the kingdom emphasized God's role in its achievement; others emphasized the role of human institutions and programs.

The eschatological or apocalyptic passages in Scripture were treated in two basic ways: one was to interpret the passages noneschatologically or nonfuturistically; the other was simply to discard or disregard them (as well as other segments of the Bible).

Those who followed the latter approach gave prominence to the analogy of kernel and husk. Although dating from a later time, the work of Harry Emerson Fosdick (1878–1969) illustrates well this approach. As Fosdick saw it, the traditional form of the doctrine that righteousness will triumph is the second coming of Christ.[5] According to this form of the doctrine, Jesus will return to earth in literal fashion in the clouds of heaven. It is not surprising that persons of the first century accepted and employed such imagery. They regarded the earth as a flat parallelogram, so it was appropriate to think of someone ascending into the clouds and descending from them. Nor is it surprising that this hope took on a messianic form, for this was a time of intense political agitation. As one nation succeeded another, the conception grew that Israel would be delivered by an earthly king who would reestablish David's kingdom. During the intertestamental period and in the Apocryphal

---

5. *The Modern Use of the Bible*, p. 105.

writings, the outlook upon the present became increasingly pessimistic. Deliverance would necessarily come through a sudden dramatic event—the day of the Lord—involving a messianic invasion of earth from heaven.

Fosdick concluded that today we cannot hold such a view, bound up as it is with an obsolete view of reality. But in rejecting this idea, we are only peeling off and discarding the husk. The kernel (the victory of righteousness upon earth) remains intact, and Fosdick continued to believe it. While the husk of the doctrine (the physical return of Jesus) was adequate for another day, a new form must be found for our time. And Fosdick had one to propose. It is not the idea of man's simply transforming human character and society by his own effort, but of God's working through Christian believers to alter society. Fosdick put it thus:

> To be ourselves of such a spirit that God can work his victory in and through us; to persuade others to be transformed by the renewing of their minds; to strive for the better organization of society that the divine purpose may be furthered, not hindered, by our economic and political life; and then to await the event in his way and time—such have been our attitude and our preaching, and they have seemed to us Christian.[6]

Consistent Eschatology

We have noted the growing consensus among liberals regarding the eschatology of the New Testament. Despite many variations they agreed that the kingdom is ethical in nature. It is here and now, within history. It is not something that will come catastrophically at some future time.

In this apparently solid front, however, cracks began to appear. Writers were suggesting that something was wrong with the liberal view. Some proposed a compromise, wedding a truly eschatological or futuristic view with the idea of the kingdom as a present ethical reality. Others, however, assayed a complete break. One of these was Johannes Weiss, who in 1892 published *Jesus' Preaching on the Kingdom of God.* In this work Weiss approached the teaching of Jesus from a totally different perspective. Instead of assuming that

---

6. Ibid., p. 110.

Jesus was talking about an ethical kingdom, he assumed that Jesus was thoroughly eschatological, or even apocalyptic and futuristic in His outlook. Instead of an ethical rule of God in the hearts of men, expanding gradually through time, the kingdom was to be introduced dramatically in the future. From this, Weiss's schema derived the name *consistent* (or thoroughgoing) *eschatology.*

If Weiss opened a crack in the wall, Albert Schweitzer (1875–1965) produced a full-fledged fissure. In two of his books, Schweitzer addressed himself explicitly to the question of eschatology. The first was *Das Abendmahl,* the second half of which was published in English as *The Mystery of the Kingdom of God.* In some ways it defined his position more clearly than did his better-known later work, *The Quest of the Historical Jesus.* Schweitzer thoroughly examined and virtually demolished the liberal "lives of Jesus" and then proposed an alternative construction. Weiss had applied the idea of consistent eschatology to the teachings of Jesus; Schweitzer, however, applied it to the New Testament as a whole.

Schweitzer is a modern example of a universal genius. Already an accomplished organist, philosopher, and New Testament scholar by the age of thirty, he then turned to medicine and became a medical missionary in Lambarene, Africa. Schweitzer had been trained in the classical liberalism of his day, but he began to see defects within it. He did not, however, return to a precritical approach to the Bible. He accepted the validity of the liberal method of critical study, but he rejected some of its conclusions. The problem stemmed from either incorrect assumptions, or incomplete and inconsistent application of the method, or both. If we open ourselves to the possibility that the New Testament is genuinely eschatological, we can explain the phenomena more adequately. If, on the other hand, we accept the liberals' assumptions and follow their method of critical Biblical study completely, we find certain inconsistencies.

Schweitzer, we noted, adopted the method of the liberal searchers for Jesus and utilized the same materials. For the most part he, like Weiss, William Wrede, and others, ignored the Fourth Gospel, regarding it as far too divergent from the Synoptics to be historically reliable. Schweitzer also used Luke's Gospel rather sparingly, feeling that in it, Paul's theology had been "read back into" the narrative. Luke was a member of Paul's circle, as the "we" passages in Acts indicate. Since Luke wrote after the period of Paul's direct influence upon him, his Gospel should probably be disregarded by anyone who wishes to get back to the life and sayings of Jesus. Schweitzer's major sources, then, were Mark and the *Logia* (sayings in Matthew), which he regarded as having been derived from something identified as Q (from the German word for "source," *Quelle).* Even Matthew's construction of the gospel facts was regarded with considerable skepticism. The sayings of Jesus reported in Matthew were treated as quite reliable, but the narrative was thought to have been influenced by later events and conceptions.

In effect, then, Schweitzer retraced the path of the searchers for the historical Jesus. He applied their method to the materials that they accepted as authentic, and his evaluation of their results was quite negative: "Whatever the ultimate solution may be, the historical Jesus of whom the criticism of the future, taking as its starting-point the problems which have been recognised and admitted, will draw the portrait, can never render modern theology the services which it claimed from its own half-historical, half-modern, Jesus."[7] We often think that the great problem of Christology is that of Christ's two natures, of God and man being combined in one person. Schweitzer felt that the problem of combining a partially historical and partially contemporary Jesus in one person is much more difficult. In fact Schweitzer felt that the two had not been combined successfully.

The problem is that the Jesus who emerges from such an endeavor is fictitious. Father George Tyrrell's famous statement comes to mind: "The Christ that Harnack sees, looking back through nineteen centuries of Catholic darkness, is only the reflection of a liberal Protestant face, seen at the bottom of a deep well."[8] Similarly Schweitzer suggested that the Jesus of whom the liberal searcher spoke and wrote had no reality at all: "The Jesus of Nazareth who came forward publicly as the Messiah, who preached the ethic of the Kingdom of God, who founded the Kingdom of Heaven upon earth, and died to give His work its final consecra-

---

7. *The Quest of the Historical Jesus: A Critical Study of Its Progress from Reimarus to Wrede,* p. 396.

8. *Christianity at the Cross-Roads,* p. 44.

tion, never had any existence. He is a figure designed by rationalism, endowed with life by liberalism, and clothed by modern theology in an historical garb."[9]

This Jesus of history is not a product of historical research at all, but of nineteenth- and twentieth-century thought. Ostensibly the attempt to get at the life of Jesus was an attempt to bring Jesus into the present, but He could not be captured in this way.

> But He does not stay; He passes by our time and returns to His own. What surprised and dismayed the theology of the last forty years was that, despite all forced and arbitrary interpretations, it could not keep Him in our time, but had to let Him go. He returned to His own time, not owing to the application of any historical ingenuity, but by the same inevitable necessity by which the liberated pendulum returns to its original position.[10]

If Jesus is to have significance for our time, it will be not by His becoming like us but by our seeing Him as He truly was. The image of Jesus as teaching simply an ethical kingdom has been destroyed—not by external criticism, not by people who take a fundamentally different approach to historical research, but by the failure of the method to account for significant internal problems. It failed because it had to ignore important data. The noneschatological, ethical interpretation of Jesus must therefore be supplanted by a thoroughly eschatological interpretation.

The noneschatological view of Jesus had failed to unlock the "mystery" of Jesus. Perhaps another key would fit better, accounting for more of the phenomena of Jesus' life and with less distortion. When the eschatological image of Jesus was projected, His life and teaching began to make good sense. While the teachings of Jesus emphasized the present dimensions of the kingdom, they also included future coming events—the coming of Jesus.

The expression "the second coming of Jesus," or His "coming again," is commonly used today. Schweitzer disliked it. It was not Jesus' term. From where He stood, it was His *coming,* and that was a *future* coming. We tend to contrast Jesus' future coming with His

---

9. *The Quest of the Historical Jesus,* p. 396.
10. Ibid., p. 397.

death: His death represented the ultimate in what is sometimes referred to as the state of humiliation; His coming is the completion of the state of exaltation which began with His resurrection and was furthered in His ascension. In Schweitzer's thinking these are not antithetical. He does not say, "He died, *but* he is coming again," but, "He dies, *and* he is coming." The former is *instrumental* to the latter. Jesus said, "I must suffer and the Son of man shall appear upon the clouds of heaven." Schweitzer saw Jesus setting His death in a temporal-causal connection with the eschatological coming of the kingdom.[11]

Some had suggested that the eschatological idea was something of an afterthought for Jesus. Thus, Jesus initially attempted to establish an earthly kingdom, and after this attempt failed, He offered instead a future, heavenly kingdom. Schweitzer found this interpretation untenable. The eschatological notion was not forced upon Jesus by external circumstances; it was not an alternative plan to which He shifted when His original strategy proved impracticable. Rather, the eschatological conception lay at the very base of His preaching, even from the beginning of His first Galilean ministry.[12] Schweitzer illustrated this with Jesus' charge to the twelve. According to the liberal, ethical interpretation of the kingdom of God, the disciples were sent forth to introduce people to the kingdom, to invite them to enter in. But if this were true, Jesus should have included in His commission to the twelve a summary of His teachings on the morality to be practiced within this kingdom, a sort of catechism for new converts.[13]

The commission, however, includes nothing of the kind. There apparently was not to be a discipling or nurturing of people. Instead, the twelve were to warn people of the nearness of the kingdom of God and to call urgently for a decision. The disciples were not to linger in a town where men did not accept the message, but to hasten on so that they could pass through all the cities of Israel before the Son of man appeared. There was urgency because the kingdom was coming, and the one point particularly stressed was repentance.[14]

---

11. *The Mystery of the Kingdom of God: The Secret of Jesus' Messiahship and Passion,* p. 80.

12. Ibid., p. 87.   13. Ibid., p. 88.   14. Ibid.

The preparation for entrance into the kingdom, said Schweitzer, is moral transformation. "Ready yourselves, repent, clean up yourselves—judgment is coming" was the substance of the disciples' message. This, however, is quite different from what Jesus would have said if the ethical view of the kingdom were correct. Instead of spreading gradually, the kingdom is coming suddenly, and with it, judgment.[15]

The value of the kingdom is infinite. Everything is to be forsaken for the sake of it. He who would gain the kingdom must be willing to break all other ties, including even those to his family. Having begun, one must not look backward. The point of Jesus' parables of the treasure in the field (Matt. 13:44) and of the pearl of great price (Matt. 13:45–46) is that, compared to the kingdom, nothing really has value.

This coming kingdom of which Jesus spoke would be different from anything that had gone before and consequently would have definite conditions of membership. Whereas the liberals thought that Jesus' ethic was the means of producing the kingdom, Schweitzer found instead that the kingdom was determined and coming and that the ethic was the means of readying oneself for entrance into it. Those who, at the coming of the kingdom, met the moral conditions would be within the kingdom; those who did not, would not be part of it.[16] This can be verified by examining such specific teachings of Jesus as the parables. The thrust of parables like that of the wise and unwise virgins and that of the faithful and unfaithful servants is, "Be ready!"

Jesus had said, "You are not far from the kingdom." The liberals interpreted this to mean, "Qualitatively you are of the correct nature; quantitatively you only need add a little to it." Schweitzer, however, understood the reference as temporal and chronological: the kingdom was almost here. Time was short. Jesus spoke of doing the works of Him who had sent Him while there was still light. Soon the darkness would come when men could no longer labor.

This kingdom, then, was future, qualitatively novel, sudden in its coming, and of infinite value. In Schweitzer's understanding of Jesus' teaching, it had one other characteristic: it was supernatural.

---

15. Ibid., pp. 94–96.   16. Ibid., pp. 97–99.

According to liberalism men would make themselves what they were to be in the kingdom and would gradually extend the kingdom into more areas of society. This, said Schweitzer, is not what Jesus taught. Man is to prepare himself by repentance to receive the character which would be brought supernaturally. The modern way, as Schweitzer termed it, was unconditional—the kingdom would grow from small beginnings and develop more and more. Jesus' way, however, was conditional—men do not work their way into the kingdom; they prepare for and receive it. All depends upon what God does. The kingdom is supermoral, and when it comes through cosmic catastrophe, all evil will be completely overcome. Jesus' teachings rest upon the assumption of a discontinuity between conditions now and conditions in the future. Thus Jesus, for example, said very little about sexual morality, for when the kingdom came that would not be a problem. Then people would neither marry nor give in marriage but would be like the angels. He did not intend to give them a way of living within the kingdom. They were to ready themselves for it, and when the kingdom came, their new character would come with it.[17]

This, then, is Schweitzer's view of Jesus' teaching. Jesus' coming would be a dramatic event, involving cosmic disturbances. The kingdom's arrival would be a definite climax, not a gradual ingression, and it would radically transform circumstances and human character. This is what Jesus believed and taught, said Schweitzer—but of course Jesus was wrong! One might to this point have considered Schweitzer virtually a fundamentalist. His description of Jesus' beliefs and teachings is very much like that of conservative, evangelical Christians. The difference comes, however, in the attitude toward Jesus' views. Whereas the fundamentalist accepts Christ's teachings as normative, Schweitzer rejected them. Schweitzer's disagreement with the liberals was not so much with their conclusions—he basically agreed with them—but with their method of reading their views back into Jesus' teaching.

An eloquent passage in which Schweitzer summarized his view of the tragic Jesus has, both because of its literary quality and the pungency of its description of the eschatological Jesus, has become perhaps the most familiar passage in his writings:

17. Ibid., pp. 99–102.

27

There is silence all around. The Baptist appears, and cries: "Repent, for the Kingdom of Heaven is at hand." Soon after that comes Jesus, and in the knowledge that He is the coming Son of Man, lays hold of the wheel of the world to set it moving on that last revolution which is to bring all ordinary history to a close. It refuses to turn, and He throws Himself upon it. Then it does turn; and crushes Him. Instead of bringing in the eschatological conditions, He has destroyed them. The wheel rolls onward, and the mangled body of the one immeasurably great Man, who was strong enough to think of Himself as the spiritual ruler of mankind and to bend history to His purpose, is hanging upon it still. That is His victory and His reign.[18]

There is, according to Schweitzer, no way to construct or reconstruct a Jesus who did not believe this. He was mistaken, but this is what He believed, and one can understand him only on this basis. Any other assumption will lead to gross distortion of the Biblical Jesus.

But what significance does such a Jesus have for us today? We have seen that one cannot accept these obsolete ideas in our modern world. And not only that, but they were not (and should not have been) held by the generation following Jesus, for His expectations did not come to pass. The significance of Jesus does not lie in our being somehow related to this historically constructed Jesus, but in our knowing Him in a mystical sort of direct encounter. Schweitzer concluded *The Quest of the Historical Jesus:*

> For that reason it is a good thing that the true historical Jesus should overthrow the modern Jesus, should rise up against the modern spirit and send upon earth, not peace, but a sword. He was not a teacher, not a casuist; He was an imperious ruler. It was because He was so in His inmost being that He could think of Himself as the Son of Man. That was only the temporally conditioned expression of the fact that He was an authoritative ruler. The names in which men expressed their recognition of Him as such, Messiah, Son of Man, Son of God, have become for us historical parables. We can find no designation which expresses what He is for us.
>
> He comes to us as One unknown, without a name, as of old, by the lake-side, He came to those men who knew Him not. He speaks to us the same word: "Follow thou me!" and

---

18. *The Quest of the Historical Jesus*, pp. 368–69.

sets us to the tasks which He has to fulfil for our time. He commands. And to those who obey Him, whether they be wise or simple, He will reveal Himself in the toils, the conflicts, the sufferings which they shall pass through in His fellowship, and, as an ineffable mystery, they shall learn in their own experience Who He is.[19]

As one serves and follows the Jesus who still comes to him in his personal experience as He came to the disciples long ago, he learns who this ineffably mysterious One is. Here in a sense is an anticipation of the later neo-orthodoxy, in which one does not gather knowledge as in objective research. The truth is subjective and personal, and one can know it only by revelation, by the initiative of the Lord. Here, however, we have a considerably more mystical tone than in most of neo-orthodoxy. Karl Barth emphasized that one has knowledge in this revelation, whereas Schweitzer accentuated the idea of ineffable mystery.

The strength of Schweitzer's work appears to lie in its negative or critical dimension. He thoroughly and accurately laid bare the shortcomings and weaknesses of the liberal noneschatological or deeschatologized views of Jesus and the kingdom. He did not do this by rejecting the liberal's basic methodology and substituting another. He met these men on their own ground. Applying their own principles of interpretation, he showed that the picture of Jesus which emerged did not fit the data, that it was inconsistent with the hypothesis proposed. Schweitzer demonstrated that the noneschatological preacher of a purely ethical kingdom never really existed. He was the product of a creative liberal imagination, a being from the nineteenth century, not the first.

Unfortunately Schweitzer's work of criticism was not matched by an equally strong, constructive alternative. Thus Schweitzer's concluding note is, to say the least, very vague and subjective. After a closely reasoned analytical argument, he turns to an almost mystical solution, suggesting that Jesus comes to us as He did to the disciples long ago. The brevity and vagueness of his statement make it difficult to determine just what he was asserting, or what his basis was for it. As a result, this part of Schweitzer's argument appears to be virtually an afterthought. As such it can scarcely serve as an adequate belief for us today.

---

19. Ibid., p. 401.

Realized Eschatology

The history of Christian theology, like that of many other things, frequently moves in a pendular fashion. One type of thinking runs its course, reaching a point of maximum acceptance and influence, and then is replaced by one that moves in an opposite direction, frequently resembling closely an earlier, supplanted view. Yet, it is seldom a total break from its immediate predecessor. Because it can scarcely avoid being influenced by what has gone before, it incorporates elements of the old.

So it was with realized eschatology, a movement identified especially with Charles H. Dodd (1884–1973), but held by others as well. It shared one characteristic with consistent eschatology: it saw the eschatological motif as permeating Scripture, and especially Jesus' teachings. However, consistent eschatology had regarded the events that Jesus anticipated as having never occurred, while Dodd said that these events had occurred. Furthermore, he saw them as occurring contemporaneously with the writing, or within the Biblical period. His view of eschatology is what is sometimes referred to as "preterist."

In general there are four ways to interpret Biblical eschatology. While these are particularly applied to distinctly apocalyptic portions of the Bible such as the Book of Revelation, they are applied to other segments as well. The *idealist* (or symbolic) interpretation detemporalizes the apocalyptic. The symbols or events it describes will not come to pass at some specific point in history, but represent and present "timeless truths," truths about the nature of reality or human existence that either are continuously present or continually recur. One does not ask of them "When?" but rather "What?" The *futurist* refers the prophetic and apocalyptic elements in the Scriptures primarily to an "end time" when all of the events will come to pass. Most of it is still future to us, as it was to those living in Biblical times. The *historicist* sees the apocalyptic as pertaining to events which at the time they were described (the Biblical period) were still future, but which have occurred and are occurring within the lifespan of the church. The *preterist* approach sees the fulfillment of the apocalyptic taking place roughly contemporaneously with the Scriptural account of it. Thus the "last times" would already have arrived when the Scripture writer described them.

Realized eschatology challenged the idea of *futurity* in connection with Jesus' teachings. He was not speaking of wholly future events that were yet unfulfilled; the "things which were to come" had *already* come. Scripture contained a sharp contrast between "this age" and "the age to come." In the Old Testament prophets this contrast focused upon the day of the Lord, which was characterized by three distinctives:[20]

1. It would be supernatural. The hidden rule of God in history would be revealed. Whereas the prophets saw God at work, using even Assyria and Babylonia, sometime in the future God would be revealed as the ruler of history; it would become apparent that this rule is divine and supernatural.

2. The day of the Lord would involve the overthrow of the powers of evil, as well as judgment on the sin of men. When the day of the Lord came, there would be justice.

3. Since the will of God for man is perfection of life in God's image and in fellowship with Him, the day of the Lord would bring a new life to those in whom His will is fulfilled. Scripture affirms this in numerous places. For example, "We shall be like him, for we shall see him as he is" (I John 3:2). In the Old Testament the same idea occurs: "And I will . . . put a new spirit within them" (Ezek. 11:19). In the New Testament the Old Testament apocalyptic symbolism recurs frequently.

According to realized eschatology there is a crucial difference between the Old and the New Testament references. While in the former the day of the Lord is future, in the latter this day has come. Dodd quoted an assortment of New Testament passages to support this contention: "The kingdom of God has come upon you" (Matt. 12:28); "This is what was spoken by the prophet Joel" (Acts 2:16); "We all . . . are being changed into his likeness from one degree of glory to another" (II Cor. 3:18); "If any one is in Christ, he is a new creation" (II Cor. 5:17); "He has delivered us from the dominion of darkness and transferred us to the kingdom of his beloved Son" (Col. 1:13); "He saved us . . . by the washing of regeneration and renewal in the Holy Spirit" (Titus 3:5); ". . . have tasted . . . the powers of the age to come" (Heb. 6:5);

---

20. Charles H. Dodd, *The Apostolic Preaching and Its Development,* pp. 142–43.

"You have been born anew, not of perishable seed but of imperishable" (I Peter 1:23); "The darkness is passing away and the true light is already shining. . . . it is the last hour" (I John 2:8, 18).

As Dodd saw it, the new age is here; God has established the kingdom. The mythological concept of the day of the Lord has been transferred to a definite historical event that has occurred, or actually to a series of such events—the ministry, death, and resurrection of Jesus Christ. Eschatology has been fulfilled or "realized." What was future at the time of Old Testament prophecies has become present. Instead of looking for two comings of Christ, we should understand that there is only one; and instead of looking for future fulfillments of Jesus' "predictions," we should interpret these "predictions" in the light of His statements that the kingdom of God is here—it is at hand. Jesus was not speaking of how it would be, but of how it was.

A particular crisis, constituted by the ministry, death, and resurrection of Jesus Christ, is interpreted in terms of the Old Testament concept. The characteristics of the day of the Lord are boldly transferred to this historical crisis. We may note how well this complex of events matches the concept of the day of the Lord.[21]

1. It is fulfillment. Mark said, "The time is fulfilled." Dodd commented, "This is the declaration which Mark inscribed over virtually the entire gospel record." Paul said in Galatians 4:4, "When the fulness ($\pi\lambda\acute{\eta}\rho\omega\mu\alpha$) of the time was come. . . ." (KJV). What more could be fulfilled? There was nothing yet to happen, or Paul would certainly not have used this particular term. This is the key to the frequent appeals (made especially by Matthew) to prophecy. The point is that the meaning of history is now summed up. The fulfillment of prophecy means that the day of the Lord has dawned.

2. The supernatural has entered history. The arm of the Lord is made bare, as the miracles in the life of Jesus demonstrate. These, like prophecy, have been used by some to prove the supernatural. In one sense this is correct, but Dodd said that the miracle stories of the Gospels correspond closely with the symbols the prophets used to depict the supernatural character of the age to come. The power was there—Jesus could say to the man, "Take up your bed

---

21. Ibid., pp. 147–49.

and walk." How could a millennium improve upon that? The kingdom had come.

3. God's power is openly manifest in the overthrow of the powers of evil. For example, when the seventy return and announce what has been accomplished, Jesus says, "I saw Satan fall like lightning from heaven" (Luke 10:18). John has Jesus saying on the eve of His death, ". . . now shall the ruler of this world be cast out" (12:31). Paul said that in the cross God triumphed over principalities and powers. If the day of the Lord includes the destruction of the powers of evil and if this took place on the cross, then that day has come.

4. The Christ-event also involves judgment of the world. In the death of Christ, said Paul, God manifested His righteousness and condemned sin in the flesh. Paul should be seen as, in effect, interpreting Jesus. Dodd placed somewhat greater confidence in Paul than did either the liberal "searchers" or Schweitzer. "This is the judgment, that the light has come into the world, and men loved darkness rather than light, because their deeds were evil" (John 3:19). In the preamble to the Fourth Gospel, the light has come into the world, and it *is shining,* and the darkness has not overcome it. This is judgment, not in some futuristic sense in which the books are opened, the evidence examined, and a verdict rendered by a judge. Men have passed judgment upon themselves by their response to the light: they "loved darkness rather than light, because their deeds were evil." Judgment is self-administered, by the response people make to the truth.

5. Eternal life, the life of the age to come, is now realized in experience. "Christ has been raised from the dead, the first fruits of those who have fallen asleep" (I Cor. 15:22), and we are raised with Him in newness of life. The fundamentalist rendition of eternal life was sometimes totally futuristic: believe, and someday you will have eternal life; you will go to live with Him forever in heaven. Jesus said, "I came that they may have life, and have it abundantly" (John 10:10). He who believes, has eternal life. It is not something to be anticipated; it is to be experienced.

Eschatology, then, is a matter of the present. Dodd gave the parables detailed examination, interpreting them in light of what had already occurred or was occurring. "The future is now" was an excellent motto for Jesus' ministry, as Dodd understood it.

We find here some parallels to the older liberal view which held that these things are not solely future. In that sense realized eschatology is something of a reaction to Schweitzer. Yet it is also a much more supernatural view than is liberalism's. Dodd saw Jesus speaking not of what would come but of what had come. Some critics suggested that Dodd had overstated his case, and he apparently accepted this criticism; in his later works he began to speak increasingly of the kingdom having *begun* rather than of its having *come,* and of *initiation* rather than *realization.* [22] Nonetheless, in Dodd's view there is not much yet to await.

The strength of realized eschatology is its tenet that much of the eschatology of which Jesus spoke was already fulfilled or being fulfilled within His time. In Christ the future had come, or at least it had begun. The tendency of some Christians to understand Scriptural eschatology in purely futuristic terms must therefore be regarded as a mistaken, perverted view of Scriptural teaching. These people miss much of the significance of the text because they are looking forward when they should be looking backward.

On the other hand, Dodd neglected some texts which cannot be regarded as already fulfilled. For example, when in the great eschatological discourse, Jesus spoke of His second coming, and when Paul reflected upon this in Thessalonians, they clearly referred to events which were (and are) still future. While the kingdom has in one sense already come, or at least begun to come, in another sense it has clearly not yet been realized. A fully adequate eschatological theory ought to account for these portions of Scripture as well. This Dodd failed to do.

---

22. *Gospel and Law: The Relation of Faith and Ethics in Early Christianity,* pp. 26–27.

Chapter 2

Bultmann and Moltmann

Existential Eschatology

In the thought of Rudolf Bultmann (1884–1976), we find a genuinely twentieth-century approach to theology. While he combined many elements from several of the preceding approaches, he constructed his thought primarily upon the philosophy of existentialism, which in many ways has been the leading philosophy of this century.

Bultmann wrote not as a systematic theologian but as a New Testament scholar. Examining the world view of the New Testament, he found much that is mythological in nature. By *myth* he meant the description of otherworldly realities in imagery drawn from this world. The New Testament writers conceived of the whole of reality as a three-storied universe. The top story is heaven, populated by God and the angels; the middle is earth, inhabited by humans; and the lowest is hell, the home base of the devil and his demonic assistants. Even on earth not all is the result of purely natural forces. Supernatural powers intervene in the "natural" flow of events. Miracles occur with considerable frequency. Evil spirits may take possession of man, causing illness. God or Satan may inspire man's thoughts and guide his actions. He may have divinely sent visions.[1]

Eschatology is a prominent part of this picture as well. The end of time is coming soon and will be marked by a great cosmic

---

1. "New Testament and Mythology," pp. 1–2.

catastrophe. The end will be inaugurated by the "woes" of the last time. The judge, the Lord Jesus, will come from heaven, riding on the clouds, to complete the work of redemption. Then men will be resurrected and judged.[2] Eschatology is set within the framework of mythology in general, and to understand Bultmann's eschatology we must first look at his general method of demythologization.

There are three ways to deal with the mythology of the New Testament. The first is simply to accept it literally, and to a large extent this is what fundamentalism does. But, said Bultmann, this is obviously impossible for modern man in view of the present scientific conception of reality. The Copernican revolution rendered it impossible for thinking, enlightened persons to regard the universe as spatial "up" and "down," or as in any way corresponding to a spatial frame of reference. Such concepts no longer have meaning. Similarly medical science has revealed that diseases are not caused by demon possession but by bacteria, viruses, and other organisms.[3] Another reason why we cannot adopt the mythical eschatology is that the parousia of Christ predicted in the New Testament never took place. History did not end within that generation, and as everyone knows, it will continue to run its course. If we do believe in an end of the world within time, we expect it in the form of a natural catastrophe (e.g., a nuclear holocaust), not of a mythical bodily return of Jesus Christ, concluded Bultmann. But, to explain this parousia in terms of some natural catastrophe is to apply criticism to the New Testament, albeit unconsciously.[4]

The second way to treat New Testament mythology is that of liberalism: reject the mythological elements of the New Testament. Liberals endeavored to retain the New Testament message, but without those elements now recognized as untenable. Bultmann called this the method of selection or subtraction. Unfortunately, he said, it is not feasible. In many cases the mythological is so closely bound to the nonmythological that they are virtually inseparable.[5]

---

2. Ibid.

3. Ibid., pp. 3–4.

4. Ibid., p. 5.

5. Ibid., pp. 9–10.

A third way of dealing with New Testament mythology is the one Bultmann believed to be superior: instead of accepting the mythology literally or rejecting it, interpret it (or perhaps more correctly, reinterpret it). He took the myths seriously, as actually conveying a message, but not literally. This process is known as demythologization, a term that leaves something to be desired because it suggests that myth is being eliminated. Rather, myth is being reinterpreted, allowing it to remain, but giving it a different character. Bultmann attempted to understand myth in terms of its existential, rather than its literal, meaning.[6]

Bultmann recognized that there have been previous efforts of sorts at demythologizing. In fact he asserted that all he had said in a negative way could have been, and indeed had been, affirmed forty years earlier. That it was necessary to go through all of this again he regarded as a sign of the bankruptcy of contemporary theology. In his day he witnessed a movement away from criticism and back to a naive acceptance of the early church's preaching.[7] Perhaps this was because some of the earlier attempts at demythologization used criticism virtually to *eliminate* this kerygma, thus lapsing into the second of the two methods described above.[8] Adolf von Harnack, for example, completely eliminated mythology: "The kingdom of God comes by coming to the individual, by entering into his soul and laying hold of it."[9] Harnack reduced the kerygma to a few basic principles of religion and ethics that are timeless and eternal, independent of the human history within which they are realized. We are capable of verifying these truths in our own experience, regardless of when we happen to live. Since Harnack understood the kerygma as nothing more than mythology, he could safely eliminate it.

We must ask, said Bultmann, what the New Testament personages, and especially the authors of the New Testament books, were trying to express. While those who first enunciated these mythical ideas may have understood them literally, these ideas definitely have a more significant meaning than this. The real meaning, which

---

6. Ibid., p. 10.
7. Ibid., p. 12.
8. Ibid., p. 13.
9. *What Is Christianity?*, p. 56.

these authors had experienced and were expressing in mythological form, is existential. If we are to capture the genuine meaning of the ideas, we must look for their existential significance.[10]

Bultmann's method rests upon a crucial distinction that runs throughout his thought and is most clearly seen in his understanding of history. He distinguished two meanings or types of history, *Historie* and *Geschichte. Historie* is the issue of what actually occurred, the factuality of space-time events. The question here is simply, "Did it happen?" One might term this, *mere history.* This is the realm of the "historical." *Geschichte,* on the other hand, is the effect or subjective impact these events have upon participants or observers. The question here would be, "What does it mean?" This is *significant history,* or the historic occurrences.[11]

Applying this distinction to the Gospels and employing his methodology of form criticism, Bultmann was quite skeptical about *Historie.* We cannot be certain that we have any saying of Jesus just as He declared it and in precisely the original setting. The Gospels were not written by impartial observers who were simply reporting information for others, but by committed Christians who were attempting to bring others to a similar commitment. In other words, they are more like propaganda, advertising, or sales literature than objective reports.

We cannot determine whether Jesus actually was crucified or resurrected. Further, the resurrection is not only uncertain from the standpoint of evidence, but also unlikely, or more correctly, incredible. What we know of the process by which dead bodies decompose makes it impossible for one who has been dead for three days to come to life again.[12] It is a sheer, physical impossibility.

What we do have in the Gospel accounts, however, is *Geschichte.* Whatever actually happened, it made a tremendous impact upon the disciples. They attempted to express this in what they wrote and did. The Gospels, therefore, are not so much a record of Jesus' sayings and deeds as a series of expressions of the

---

10. "New Testament and Mythology."

11. Ibid., p. 37.

12. Ibid., p. 8.

disciples' subjective experiences. Myth expresses man's convictions of something beyond. The origin and purpose of this world are to be sought not within but beyond it. Further, man is not his own lord. He is dependent upon this world and upon powers beyond it from which he can be freed. Hence myth is an expression of man's self-understanding. Its meaning is not found in events that once took place or that will occur some time in the future. It has a timelessness, expressing the nature of human existence *as such.*[13]

Bultmann brought to his interpretation of the New Testament the existential philosophy of Martin Heidegger. He considered Heidegger's analysis of the ontological structure of being to be a secularized, philosophical version of the New Testament view of human existence.[14] For Heidegger, anxiety is the chief characteristic of man's being. Man is continually confronted with the decision between past and future, whether to lose himself in the world of things and thereby lose his individuality to the masses (inauthentic existence), or to achieve authentic existence by surrendering all security and committing himself unreservedly to the future. Bultmann accepted the basic structure of this view but insisted that there is a crucial difference between existentialism and the New Testament message: according to the former, man achieves authentic existence by freeing himself from captivity to the transitory and tangible through his own decision; according to the latter, man cannot free himself from himself by his own effort—this must come as a gift.[15]

Let us now observe how Bultmann reinterpreted a couple of significant doctrines on the basis of this approach. The cross is both historical and mythological. The mythological interpretation of the cross is what Bultmann called a "mixture of sacrificial and juridical analogies"; its demythologized meaning is otherwise. As an historical event *(Historie),* the cross is simply the fact of the crucifixion of Jesus of Nazareth; as an historic event *(Geschichte),* however, the cross is the judgment of the world, the liberating judgment over man, "the judgment of ourselves as fallen creatures enslaved to the powers of the 'world.'" To believe in the cross,

---

13. Ibid., pp. 10–11.

14. Ibid., pp. 24–25.

15. Ibid., p. 27.

then, is to take the cross upon oneself, to allow oneself to be crucified with Christ.[16] The prime text for a demythologized understanding of the crucifixion is Galatians 2:20, "I have been crucified with Christ." The real meaning of the cross is not something that happened centuries ago; it is something that applies to me here and now. The question is not what we can determine about occurrences in Jesus' life long ago (i.e., whether He was put to death). The really significant issue is whether I have put to death my lusts, my self-striving, my attachment to the here and now.

Bultmann necessarily handled the resurrection somewhat differently since, as we noted above, it cannot be considered *Historie*. The significance *(Geschichte)* of the resurrection derives from the cross. If the cross is the declaration of judgment upon man, then the resurrection is the assurance of victory. The cross and the resurrection are eschatological events not as past occurrences but as events included in the kerygma. Only in preaching does Christ encounter us as the crucified and risen One. The event described in the kerygma reoccurs in the experience of the hearer. We come to life anew, we take hope, we trust in the future.[17]

Bultmann took this same type of approach to eschatology. He examined Jesus' preaching and teaching about the last things, and he, in common with consistent eschatologists and in contrast both to the authors of liberal "lives of Jesus" and to realized eschatologists, found that Jesus had definitely believed in a future kingdom of God. Careful research, he said, has shown "that Jesus undoubtedly understood the kingdom of God as future and expected its coming and therewith the judgment and eschatological consummation in the near time—if not in the next time, then in the lifetimes of the present generation."[18] This was not to deny that Jesus saw the ἔσχατον as bound up with the present. In His own person the future eschatological judge, the Son of man, was already present. Jesus saw an interval between the present and the future. This was related to His expectation of His death and resurrection, and, after a time, His parousia. Clearly Jesus taught a mythological

16. Ibid., p. 36.
17. Ibid., p. 38.
18. *"Zur Eschatologischen Verkündigung Jesu,"* p. 271.

eschatology—a view we cannot accept because it did not come to pass as Jesus said it would.

Eschatology, like history, is detemporalized. While narrative in the Gospels ostensibly reports events that have occurred at some point in the past, eschatological references appear to predict events that will occur in the future. Like narrative, however, eschatological references must be seen as an expression of man's understanding of existence as he experiences it at the time. Unlike the realized eschatologists, for whom the meaning of eschatological references is their fulfillment at the time of their utterance, Bultmann found the meaning of them in their fulfillment in the believer's present experience.

Some see this effort to redefine eschatology as a deviation from Biblical teaching, a virtual rejection of Biblical authority. This is not the case, claimed Bultmann. Demythologization was, in fact, begun by the Biblical writers.[19] Paul, for example, did not regard salvation as primarily future, to be realized in another world, but as a present occurrence: "If any one is in Christ, he is a new creation; the old has passed away, behold, the new has come" (II Cor. 5:17); "Death is swallowed up in victory" (I Cor. 15:54); "Behold, now is the acceptable time [about which Isaiah spoke]; behold, now is the day of salvation" (II Cor. 6:2). What Paul began was carried even further by John, for whom the coming and departure of Jesus are eschatological events. John did not consign judgment to a future point; it is occurring at present: "And this is the judgment, that the light has come into the world, and men loved darkness rather than light, because their deeds were evil" (John 3:19). The evil forces of the world are also being presently judged: "Now is the judgment of this world, now shall the ruler of this world be cast out" (John 12:31). Bultmann commented: "For John the resurrection of Jesus, Pentecost and the *parousia* of Jesus are one and the same event, and those who believe have already eternal life."[20] Bultmann cited numerous passages in John to support this contention: "He who believes in him is not condemned; he who does not believe is condemned already" (3:18); "He who believes in the Son has eternal life; he who does not obey the Son shall not see life,

---

19. *Jesus Christ and Mythology,* p. 31.

20. Ibid., p. 33.

but the wrath of God rests upon him" (3:36); "Truly, truly, I say
to you, the hour is coming, and now is, when the dead will hear the
voice of the Son of God, and those who hear will live" (5:25); "I
am the resurrection and the life; he who believes in me, though he
die, yet shall he live, and whoever lives and believes in me shall
never die" (11:25–26).[21]

Scripture writers extended this demythologizing to particular
instances as well. Jewish eschatological expectations included the
coming of a personal Antichrist in the end times, as described for
example in II Thessalonians 2:7–12. John, by contrast, saw this
expectation fulfilled by false teachers (I John 4:3). The point,
however, is not that these contemporary teachers fulfilled the prediction within John's lifetime, therefore concluding this matter
once and for all, but that an anti-Christian *spirit* is to be found at
all times, against which Christians should ever be on guard.

Eschatology was for Bultmann almost like a parable. No one,
presumably, takes the parable of the prodigal son as a literal event
that occurred somewhere in time and space. It is a story about
man, not about *a man,* and I am man. Further, it is not a picture of
how we are at a particular time, but of how we are all the time.
One does not properly ask the name of the prodigal son, or where
the far country was, or what variety of grain he ate. One does not
verify the parable by establishing its historicity, but by examining
his own subjective experience. So it is with Bultmann's view of
eschatology. One does not ask, "Will it happen this way?" but,
"Am I experiencing in my own existence the truths of which this
speaks?"

We have in Bultmann's writing a rather radical reconstruction of
the nature of eschatology. In particular we see the effect upon
doctrine of adopting existential philosophy and molding one's
theology upon it. Existentialism rejects substances or essences.
Salvation, on existentialist grounds, is not something that has
occurred once for all in static fashion. Rather, it must be dynamic,
relational, recurring.

Perhaps the greatest strength of this type of eschatology is the
relevance it gives to eschatological teachings. Instead of referring to
something that happened once long ago or is yet to transpire, the

---

21. Ibid., pp. 33–34.

teachings of eschatology are true in the present. They have immediate pertinence. They are not for persons who lived in the past or who will live sometime in the future. They are for me, living *now*. They consequently are preachable. Certainly Jesus and Paul addressed their messages to the readers and hearers of their time, intending their messages to guide their audiences' lives at that time.

Bultmann also correctly noted that the message must in some sense participate in and be expressed in the thought forms of its time and must utilize concepts and expressions drawn from sense experience. Thus, to convey the greatness, beauty, and glory of heaven, the Scripture author quite naturally employed the symbolism of streets paved with gold. Perhaps all interpreters of Scripture, even the most conservative, have recognized that not all of Scripture should be interpreted in the most literal fashion possible.

At points, however, this treatment of eschatology is clearly defective. Bultmann's use of Scripture, for example, is highly selective. There certainly are elements in the writings of both Paul and John that regard the doctrines of eschatology as something true of the present moment. On the other hand, Bultmann carefully avoided passages that must be taken in a futuristic sense. While implicitly conceding this in his reference to Paul's statement in II Thessalonians about the personal Antichrist, Bultmann never explicitly acknowledged it.

Further, Bultmann's view seems contrary to the dynamics of human psychology. Thus, existential experience *(Geschichte)* seems for Bultmann to be separable from the questions of the actual occurrence of the events *(Historie)* or the "truth" of the doctrines. We should note, however, that although the questions of *Historie* may be difficult or even impossible to answer, they apparently were not so for the first generation of believers. They claimed to have observed these matters firsthand (I John 1:1) or, as in the case of Luke (Luke 1:1–4), to have engaged in rather painstaking historical inquiry into the truth of these matters. For them the transforming experience was not independent of the question of the truth of the events.

Indeed Paul seems in one case to deny rather explicitly that one could have the *Geschichte* without the *Historie:* "If Christ has not been raised, your faith is futile and you are still in your sins. Then those also who have fallen asleep in Christ have perished. If for this life only we have hoped in Christ, we are of all men most to be pitied." (I Cor. 15:17–19) *Geschichte* without *Historie?* Hardly!

Although Bultmann would undoubtedly brand the following idea rationalistic, I believe experience sustains it: when real crisis occurs, a person needs to know if his hope rests upon reality or imagination. This means that, as the New Testament doctrines are stated, the experience of victory over death and fear, for example, cannot be separated from the question of whether the resurrection actually occurred in the past or will occur in the future.

The Theology of Hope

In the mid-1960s a new theology appeared that strongly emphasizes eschatology, not as *one* of the most important doctrines of the Christian faith, nor even as *the* most important doctrine, but as the whole of theology, the framework or mood within which all theology is to be conducted. It was quickly labeled the theology of hope and has been particularly identified with Jürgen Moltmann, now professor of theology at the University of Tübingen. Others have contributed to the new eschatological emphasis at this time as well. Among these are Wolfhart Pannenberg, Moltmann's colleague at Wuppertal; Walter Kreck, his colleague at Bonn; Wolf-Dieter Marsch, his close friend and fellow student at Göttingen; Gerhard Sauter; and Johannes Metz, the Roman Catholic theologian. While there has been mutual stimulation between Moltmann and each of these men, and while they are occasionally linked with him as members of a movement, their cooperation and agreement of thought are relatively fragmentary.[22]

To understand this theology, one must see it within the context of both the personal experiences of Moltmann and the broader cultural influences as well. Moltmann, born in 1926, is part of the young generation of Germans who lived through the Second World War. He saw the German state and all its institutions collapse. He was incarcerated in an English prisoner-of-war camp until repatriated in 1948. His time in the camp had particular influence upon

22. M. Douglas Meeks, *Origins of the Theology of Hope,* pp. 1–2.

him. He noted (as have several other prisoners who have published accounts of their experiences)[23] the difference that hope makes, even for physical survival: "But basically we were neither skeptical nor resigned. Of course, we were weighed down by a dark feeling of guilt and grief. But we returned to Germany determined that now and forever things should be different, more humane and democratic. Perhaps, behind the barbed wire, we had discovered the power of a hope which sought something new, not merely a return to the old conditions."[24]

Returning home in 1948, Moltmann had a hope for a more humane Germany and for a liberating church of Christ. At the University of Göttingen he studied under Gerhard von Rad, Ernst Käsemann, Hans Joachim Iwand, Ernst Wolf, and Otto Weber. He was particularly impressed by the theology of Karl Barth. After studying Barth's *Church Dogmatics* for a time, he concluded that there could never be another new systematic theology because Barth had said everything. In 1957 the Dutch theologian Arnold A. van Ruler introduced Moltmann to eschatology. It was through reading the Marxist philosopher Ernst Bloch, however, that he was exposed to and challenged by the concept of hope. He wrote:

> My first impression was: Why has Christian theology let this theme slip away from it—a theme which certainly is its own? What has happened to the primitive Christian spirit of hope? Then I began work on the "theology of hope" and all at once the loose ends of biblical theology, of the theology of the apostolate and the Kingdom of God, and of philosophy, merged into a pattern for a tapestry in which everything matched.[25]

A good place to begin the examination of Moltmann's eschatological theology is to note its apologetical nature. It is an attempt to show the pertinence of the Christian faith by relating it in some definite way to questions being asked by the secular world. He described the crisis of Christian theology in a journal article en-

---

23. E.g., Langdon B. Gilkey, *Shantung Compound* (New York: Harper and Row, 1966); and Viktor E. Frankl, *Man's Search for Meaning* (New York: Washington Square, 1963).

24. "Politics and the Practice of Hope," p. 288.

25. Ibid., p. 289.

titled "Hope and History." He noted that many believe Christian theology to have become irrelevant, to have become introverted and individualistic, out of contact with reality. This wide field of difficulties presents a new challenge for theology. The challenge can be met only by reorganizing the theological system and re-orienting the entire theological endeavor. Two experiences under-score this new situation.

The first is conversations with modern atheists, humanists, and Marxists, in which one always arrives at the recognition of a deep schism of the modern age. In the past two centuries the Christian faith has increasingly become a faith in God without hope for the future of the world. At the same time, because of the need for hope, a secular type of hope has arisen, a secular hope for the future of the world—but without faith in God. This is the result of Christianity's failure to meet an inevitable need of man. Thus, Christianity has a God without a future, and atheism has a future without God. The messianic hopes "emigrated from the church" and became invested in progress, evolution, and revolutions. The church was left with only a half-truth. The question is, Should there be a parting of ways in history, with faith aligning itself with the past and unfaith with the future? He answered: "I think that we can overcome this present dilemma only if Christians begin to remember the 'God of Hope,' as He is witnessed to in the promis-sory history of the Old and New Testaments, and thus begin to assume responsibility for the personal, social, and political prob-lems of the present."[26]

The other experience is the emergence of "one world." While in the past each national and racial group could have its own history in relative isolation from the rest of the world, we have now reached a stage in the world's history where we are capable of annihilating the entire human race. If mankind survives, it will only be in a new community. The future will therefore not be a mere continuation of the past, with its multiplicity of histories. We have had many pasts but will have only one future. In the words of Benjamin Franklin, "We must all hang together—or we will all hang separately." We therefore have arrived at the leap from the quanti-ties of history to a new quality of history.[27]

---

26. "Hope and History," p. 370.   27. Ibid., p. 371.

This then is one side of the dilemma and crisis of Christianity: the crisis of relevance. The other is the crisis of Christianity's identity. Moltmann is concerned lest Christianity, in attempting to relate to the world's quest for hope, compromise and accommodate its true nature. In the interest of establishing a point of contact with contemporary historical existence, much modern theology has tended to be so culture-affirming that it has lost the genius of the Christian message. Moltmann, on the other hand, insists that theology stress the negative and contradictory elements of contemporary historical existence.

The relevance of theology depends upon its view of the resurrection of the crucified Christ. Christianity can show itself to be credible and relevant only by "discovering its inner truth and then orienting its life, both practically and theoretically, in terms of the one who makes the church the Christian church, who makes faith Christian faith, and so makes theology Christian theology."[28]

Out of such experiences as these, Moltmann formulated the basic orientation of his theology. What he says, in effect, is that when most true to its essential nature, Christianity is basically and radically oriented to the future, and so to hope, and consequently addresses itself to the questions being posed by mankind.

The theology of hope applies the eschatological conception to the whole of theology. Traditionally eschatology has been one of the loci of systematic theology. It has generally been the last of the topics, so that the last things were literally the last things treated. They often were handled as a sort of appendix to Christian theology—virtually dispensable, as it were. Since theology professors have often found themselves behind schedule in their lecturing, they have often given eschatology rather scanty treatment. The impression has been conveyed, almost subliminally: eschatology is unimportant. In contrast to this, Moltmann regards eschatology as a spirit, an outlook, a framework within which all of theology is to be conducted.

Much of theology has been concerned with the status of God's being, discussing it in terms of either His immanence or His transcendence. Transcendence represents God as far removed, the "God beyond us." God is so lofty and untouchable that He cannot

---

28. "The Crucified God," pp. 279–80.

be conceived. He is to be thought of cosmologically, identified with the vast cosmos. The immanent view of God pictures Him as close to us, identified with us, as "God within us," relating Him to psychological experience. Images of God emerge from every flower and every breeze. Both the God beyond us and the God within us are discredited, however, says Moltmann, because reality is neither cosmos nor pure subjectivity, but history.[29] In ancient Israel reality was thought of as history, not as cosmos or inner experience. Consequently God is conceived of on this historical model as well. He is the God of the promises and the historical guidance toward fulfillment, the God of the coming kingdom. His place is thus defined not in relationship to space but to time. He is not "beyond us" or "in us," but "in front of us" and "ahead of us." The future is the mode of God's being.

This is also the model for understanding the Bible. Reality, or the world, is thought of as history, and God is thought of as the future of history. God's future, however, is never pure future but is preceded by a history of promises and anticipations. A promise is an announcement of a reality that has not yet arrived. Israel's history of traditions reveals an alternating process of realization and reinterpretation. The hopes are fulfilled, but not completely. The new reality necessitates a new interpretation of hopes. In particular, Jesus announced the arrival of the future by bringing eschatological freedom into the present. We have in the Easter event a focus of universal hope.

Christ is the anticipation of the future of God, especially in the symbol of the resurrection. Here is the reality-prolepsis of the $\check{\varepsilon}\sigma\chi\alpha\tau\sigma\nu$: the presence of the future of one particular person, exclusively in the crucified Christ.[30] He has been raised from the dead and now lives in the future of God. In addition the gospel is also word-prolepsis. The gospel makes manifest the universal meaning inherent in the Christ-event. What has happened to Him is "for" us all and ahead of us all. It is also the forerunner of His universal appearance, for it stands between His resurrection and His appearance in glory.[31]

---

29. "Theology as Eschatology," p. 9.

30. Ibid., p. 20.

31. Ibid., p. 21.

The resurrection of Christ is the beginning and also the anticipation of the ultimate liberation of the world. The world is to be transformed. The gospel does not merely announce this fact; it actually mediates or brings about the hope. We can speak of it as a sacrament of hope. Since Christ is the future brought into the present, we must ask further how He is present to us today. He is present verbally and spiritually when the congregation is commissioned with the Word and when it fulfills its mission in the world of need.[32]

The church, then, is called to mediate the presence of Christ, who in turn mediates the future of God. But how do we mediate this hope? It is not by merely waiting passively, or even by announcing what is to come. The community has been called upon to bring about that future: "We are construction workers and not only interpreters of the future whose power in hope as well as in fulfillment is God. This means that Christian hope is a creative and militant hope in history. The horizon of eschatological expectation produces here a horizon of ethical intentions which, in turn, gives meaning to the concrete historical initiatives."[33]

The Christian is someone who hopes in the future of God and the ultimate liberation of the world. He cannot, however, passively wait for this future;[34] he must seek it, strive for it, bring it into the present. In view of the reality of hope and the future, and of the liberating and unifying nature of the future, it is not a future for the church or the soul alone. It is an all-encompassing future, able to mediate faith to earthly needs.

What is now needed, therefore, is a political theology that seeks to transform the world.[35] Ethics is not an appendix to dogmatics or a consequence of faith. Faith itself has a messianic context.[36] The Christian hope must be creative and militant. The kingdom does not simply lie in readiness, until the passage of time, so that we wait for it and leave the present as it is. We must bring the kingdom into being.

---

32. Ibid., pp. 35–36.
33. "Hope and History," p. 384.
34. Ibid.
35. Ibid.
36. Ibid.

The great problem of the older or cosmological theology, which related God to the cosmos "out there," is the problem of evil: if God is good and powerful, how can there be evil in the world? The aim of this theology is theodicy, that is, to justify God. This is still a problem for theology today, but the solution lies in a very different direction. Instead of reflection or contemplation, which leads to explanation, political theology aims at action, which actually *transforms* the problematical. In political theology the future of God is mediated in the world-changing powers of man. The old question, Why does God not do something about the obvious evil in the world if He is so good and powerful? is changed to, If we are mediators of the future of a powerful and loving God, what will we do about evil in the world?[37]

While we are not merely to wait passively for the arrival of a fixed and final future, yet the future is not simply something we anticipate as the result of our labors. "It is unreal to anticipate and work for the future if this future does not come toward us."[38] If the future is identical with the successes of our activity, it will be a pathetic future, for our actions are as ambivalent as we ourselves insofar as we are historical beings. We move toward the future, and it moves toward us. The future has value above and beyond the attained and the attainable, and this is related to and derived from the resurrection of the crucified Christ.

A number of most commendable features appear in this somewhat unusual theology. The first is that every theology has some central, integrating motif, some pivotal point around which all its parts revolve, and Moltmann is to be commended for developing his explicitly and self-consciously, not accidentally. He has made an effort to develop it thoroughly, not merely as an afterthought.

Another way of stating this is to say that Moltmann has recognized the organic character of theology. It is not merely a collection of doctrines, a loose bundle of topics. There is a connection, for example, between the view of God and the view of man.

Moltmann has tied the whole idea of the future into his ethics. Thus, belief and practice are but two aspects of the same truth, not

---

37. "Theology as Eschatology," pp. 46–47.

38. "Hope and History," p. 385.

two separate realms. Man is motivated to bring about what he believes will come to pass.

Further, Moltmann has discerned the pervasive presence of the eschatological in the Bible and especially in the Gospels, and he has striven to do justice to it. Like Albert Schweitzer he has realized that the eschatological so interpenetrates the rest of Christianity's themes that one cannot extricate, eliminate, or ignore it without ruining the whole.

On the negative side, however, there are certain problems. First, while the eschatological theme is powerfully present within Scripture, it is not the only motif. One could equally well construct a theology oriented primarily toward past occurrences in history, or the past activity of God. "Already but not yet" is one way of interpreting the message. "Still but no longer" might be equally legitimate. Because of his choice of motif Moltmann must be selective rather than comprehensive, and a theology should be comprehensive.

Second, there is a certain vagueness about this theology at the very points where it ought to be most precise. It is not at all clear just what the activity of the church is to be, or what this humanizing effect will be. There is considerable ambiguity as to the extent to which the hope Moltmann proclaims and calls for is this-worldly, a new society to be realized here on earth, and the extent to which it is otherworldly, something to be experienced after this life in some heavenly realm. As it stands, it constitutes a well-supported and clearly enunciated call to the church to exercise its influence in transforming our world, in bringing about the future; but just what this future will be like, or what it is that the church is to do, is far from clear.

Part 2

Millennial Views

Chapter 3

Postmillennialism

While the eschatological scheme known as postmillennialism is not widely held at present, it has had a rather significant influence within the church during long periods of its history, and within the last one hundred years it has at times been the dominant position.

Overview of Postmillennialism

A brief glimpse at several basic motifs will give us insight into this way of viewing the last things.

The first theme is that the kingdom of God is primarily a present reality; it is here in earthly fashion. The kingdom is not a realm, a domain over which the Lord reigns. It is, more correctly, the rule of Christ in the hearts of men. Wherever men believe in Jesus Christ, commit themselves to Him, and obey Him, the kingdom is present. It is not something to be introduced cataclysmically at some future time.[1]

Second, the postmillennialist expects a conversion of all the nations prior to Christ's return.[2] The preaching of the gospel will be effective. This will not be a human accomplishment, achieved through great skill or finely honed methodology, but a divine accomplishment, achieved through the Holy Spirit's convicting and

---

1. James H. Snowden, *The Coming of the Lord: Will It Be Premillennial?*, pp. 64–66.

2. Loraine Boettner, *The Millennium*, p. 22.

regenerating men. Not necessarily one hundred percent of the populace will be converted; substantially all persons in each of the areas and nations of the world will, however, come to believe. Worldwide revival will take place, whether rapidly or gradually. This Christianization of the world is generally thought of in an evangelical framework. The conversion of individual Christians, believing a gospel of salvation by grace through faith, will bring about this transformation of the world. Personal decision and belief constitute the fulcrum upon which new birth takes place.

A third tenet of postmillennialism is the expectation of a long period of earthly peace termed the millennium.[3] As more and more persons submit themselves to the Lord's plan and begin to practice the teachings and way of life that He established, peace will be the natural result. This is true first of relationships among nations. Here is a truly revolutionary concept, for within recorded history worldwide peace has prevailed, on the average, only about once in fifteen years! A moment's reflection on the developments of the twentieth century will reveal that genuine peace, prevailing throughout the world, is indeed rare. Not only will conflict among nations cease, but so will friction among social classes and races. Labor disputes presumably will end. Racial conflict will cease, dissolving into harmony among whites, blacks, Indians, Chicanos, and others. Even religious turmoil and denominational competition will become a thing of the past. Here is the fulfillment of the prediction that the wolf and lamb will lie down together (Isa. 11:6). He who said, "Peace I leave with you; my peace I give to you" (John 14:27), will fulfill that promise, and on a broad scale. He who is called the Prince of Peace (Isa. 9:6) will prove that He deserves that designation.

It should be noted that the postmillennialist is not literalistic about the length of the millennium: the millennium is a long period of time, not necessarily one thousand calendar years.[4] Its length would be difficult to reckon anyway because the millennium has no clear point of beginning. There will not one day be a

---

3. Snowden, *The Coming of the Lord*, pp. 257–63; Boettner, *The Millennium*, p. 53.

4. Boettner, *The Millennium*, p. 14.

condition of peace that was completely absent the previous day; the kingdom will arrive by degrees.

This, then, is the fourth distinctive motif: the gradual growth of the kingdom.[5] An earlier millennialism, like the premillennialism of our day, held that the millennial reign would begin in a sudden, dramatic fashion, through the visible, bodily return of the Lord. The postmillennial conception, on the other hand, is that the continuing spread of the gospel will increasingly introduce the kingdom.

It should also be noted that the difference between the millennial age and other ages in the life of the church is not qualitative but quantitative. Some postmillennialists have the millennium cover the entire period of the church. Those who do not, however, see the present age simply blending into the millennial age. Marriage, the family, and human birth will still be present. There will still be economic, social, and educational problems, but their most unpleasant features will be greatly modified and even eliminated.

Thus the distinction between premillennialism and postmillennialism is more than that between "before" and "after."[6] For the premillennialist the millennium is a quality of existence very different from other ages, even a different type of world. For the postmillennialist it differs from the present age only in degree.

Fifth, at the end of the millennium there will be a time of apostasy and a flare-up of evil occurring in connection with the coming of Antichrist. Loraine Boettner has suggested that God may permit this limited manifestation of evil to show anew and more clearly what an awful thing sin is and how much it deserves punishment.[7] It is understandable that those who have spent virtually their entire life in an environment of righteousness would scarcely be able to believe that sin, the devil, and his followers are as bad as they are said to be, or that they deserve such ultimate punishment as consignment to hell.

A sixth point of postmillennialism is that the millennium will end with the personal, bodily return of Christ.[8] The postmillennial

---

5. Snowden, *The Coming of the Lord,* pp. 72–85.

6. Boettner, *The Millennium,* p. 19.

7. Ibid., p. 69.

8. Charles Hodge, *Systematic Theology,* 3:792–800.

concept of the second coming is not different from that of other millennial views except in its chronological relationship to the millennium.

A seventh belief, a corollary of certain others, is that the Lord's return will be followed immediately by the resurrection of all—righteous and unrighteous—and the judgment of all, and their assignment to one of two ultimate and permanent states.[9]

One other element, found in the thought of some but not all postmillennialists, is that the Jewish nation will be converted. This is not the idea taught by some premillennialists that God's covenant is basically with the Jews and that after an interlude of dealing with the church, God will reinstate Israel to its special, favored position. Rather, it is a belief that certain prophecies which must yet be fulfilled promise that large numbers of Jews will be converted and will enter the church in the same fashion as do any believers today.

History of Postmillennialism

For the first two or three centuries of its existence, the church was largely millenarian, regarding the thousand years of Revelation eschatologically and futuristically. The church believed that Jesus would reign on earth in the future. This reign would be introduced by a definite event, probably the Lord's second coming. Sometimes this millennium was depicted rather vividly, which gave rise to something called chiliasm, a highly imaginative understanding of the earthly, thousand-year period. Sometimes chiliasm was very physical and literal in its understanding of the earthly bliss of believers.[10] This view was especially popular during the period of the church's persecution, when it seemed unlikely that the church would succeed in its effort to win the world to Christ by preaching the gospel. If the church was to be victorious, there would have to occur some dramatic, cataclysmic, supernatural reversal of the course of things.

One of the first to challenge this view was Tyconius (d. 390?), an African Donatist. He introduced an interpretation

---

9. Ibid., pp. 837ff.

10. J. A. MacCulloch, "Eschatology," p. 388.

of Revelation 20 that in various forms (especially as modified by Augustine) dominated exegesis of that passage for approximately the next thirteen centuries.[11]

Tyconius rejected the strictly eschatological view of Revelation 20 according to which it describes a purely future reign of Christ. He did this in such a way, however, that the eschatological hope was not completely lost. He expected the end to come, and in the year 380. Because we do not know his exact death date, we do not know if Tyconius survived the year 380 or what happened to his view when Christ did not return during that year.

The millennium refers to the present age. If Christ was to come in 380, then the millennium would precede it. It is a period in which, with divine help, the saints not only are not overcome by sin but are triumphant. In Tyconius's understanding the first resurrection of Revelation 20, which introduces the millennium, is from the death of sin to the life of righteousness. Those who participate in the first resurrection are those who have been born again, and this new birth takes place through baptism. The first resurrection is therefore a spiritual resurrection: it is the new birth. The millennial rule of the church was seen by Tyconius as lasting until the end of the age, or until 380. Christ was reigning right then. The throne of Christ's glory is the incarnation. It is in His incarnate body that He sits at the right hand of power and reigns. His rule is in the church, and it is present, not future. The reign of Christ is not to begin at His coming; it has already begun. The souls of the righteous in Revelation 20 are those who die with Christ in present affliction. They have died prior to the physical resurrection, for only their souls are mentioned. If these shared in the corporal rule, they would surely have bodies. The millennial rule extends from Christ's passion to His parousia and is shared in by the dead as well as the living. The blessed are those who maintain their baptism, for as the first death is due to sin, the first resurrection is due to the remission of sin.

Tyconius did not interpret the word *millennium* literally, seeing the rule of Christ only as an extended period of time. Some were

---

11. Hans Bietenhard, "The Millennial Hope in the Early Church," pp. 28–29.

more literalistic, believing that an actual one thousand years were involved, and they became very excited in their expectations as the year 1000 approached.

Augustine (354–430) popularized and promulgated Tyconius's view, despite the facts that Tyconius was a Donatist and that Augustine was the arch opponent of Donatism. Augustine too had once understood the millennium as a universal Sabbath replete with spiritual joys, but he had abandoned that futuristic interpretation, his main reason being the wild exaggerations and crude ideas in the chiliasts' descriptions of the millennium.

Like Tyconius, Augustine saw the church as already in the millennium. The one thousand years either date from the time of John to the end, or they cover the whole of the present age. Augustine cited such passages as Mark 3:27: "But no one can enter a strong man's house and plunder his goods, unless he first binds the strong man; then indeed he may plunder his house." The strong man, said Augustine, is Satan. His goods represent Christians whom he formerly had under his rule. He is bound, shut up in the abyss, so as to be kept away from Christians. Satan, then, is bound during the whole period from the first coming of Christ to the second and is therefore unable to deceive the nations of which the church is constituted. At the end of this age, he will be loosed to test the church and then will be finally and completely subjugated.[12]

It is not difficult to understand why this picture of the millennium appealed to Augustine, living in the time in which he did. He was undoubtedly affected by the "establishment" of the catholic church. A series of events culminating in the conversion of the emperor Constantine in 312 and his granting tolerance to Christianity gradually made Christianity virtually the official religion of the empire. It appeared that without any miraculous interposition of God, the church had attained a position of supremacy. As the old Roman Empire, which had been the enemy of the church, was tottering to its fall, the church seemingly was about to step into its inheritance. It was taking over the political functions of the empire. This led Augustine to idealize the political side of the catholic church. He was the first theologian to identify the catholic church, in its visible, empirical form, with the kingdom of God.[13]

---

12. Ibid., p. 29. 13. Adolf von Harnack, "Millennium," p. 317.

While the exact form of this view was altered somewhat (it was sometimes difficult to distinguish from what we call amillennialism) it prevailed for a long time. As the Middle Ages developed, it seemed increasingly that only fringe groups and cranks viewed the millennium as a future event. What we know today as premillennialism came more and more under the suspicion of heresy.[14] Many major denominations eventually incorporated postmillennialism into their creeds. The Augsburg and Westminster Confessions are basically postmillennial. Lutheran, Presbyterian, and Reformed groups have tended to follow this position. The great Princeton school of theology of the nineteenth- and early-twentieth-centuries, represented by the Hodges and Benjamin B. Warfield, staunchly presented this system.[15]

For the most part classic postmillennialists believed that the reign of Christ will become worldwide through the preaching of the gospel of personal conversion. Some postmillennialists, however, believed in a less spiritual kingdom and hence in a less spiritual gospel. The kingdom is a literal kingdom. These people practiced what is sometimes called the Social Gospel, according to which the world will be transformed from the outside in, rather than vice versa. As the structures of society are altered and the economic distribution rearranged, persons' behavior and character will change too. Some who were of a more liberal persuasion stressed the place of human effort in this process more than they did the place of God's Spirit. They saw the kingdom being introduced largely through agencies and movements outside what is strictly defined as the church. Some Christians in Germany even saw Kaiser Wilhelm's war policy as one means of God's grace, and in the 1930s some supported Nazism as the work of God.[16] Karl Barth contended that such a view failed to distinguish evil from good, the demonic from the divine. In fact, the theological end of the nineteenth century could be dated August 1914, when Barth saw on a list of German intellectuals who were endorsing the Kaiser's policies the names of several of his theological teachers. We should observe,

---

14. MacCulloch, "Eschatology," p. 388.

15. Boettner, *The Millennium,* pp. 10–11.

16. Karl Barth, *How I Changed My Mind* (Richmond: John Knox, 1966), pp. 21, 45.

however, that such persons represented the fringe element of post-millennialism. Most postmillennialists regarded the establishment of the earthly reign of Christ as supernatural in character.

Postmillennialism has suffered a sharp decline in popularity in the past fifty to sixty years. In large part this has resulted more from historical than exegetical considerations. Certain developments seemed to supply empirical evidence that the millennium was not arriving. As we will note later, the connection between these developments and the abandonment of postmillennialism was more psychological than logical. Nonetheless, the effect was there. Today postmillennialists are, if not an extinct species, at least an endangered species. As Boettner observed, however, other millennial views have had their ups and downs as well.[17] This is particularly true of premillennialism, which was "down" during the long centuries of the Middle Ages. It may well be that postmillennialism will become popular again.

Tenets of Postmillennialism

Having considered briefly the history of postmillennialism, let us now look at the basic tenets of the system, together with the arguments advanced in support of them.

The Spread of the Gospel

Crucial to the whole approach is the successful preaching of the gospel. The message will be taken worldwide and will meet with a favorable reception. Thus the church militant of today is becoming the church triumphant of tomorrow. Charles Hodge (1797–1878) offered several arguments to support this contention.[18]

First, prophecies in the Old Testament create this expectation. One prophecy is located in Isaiah 45:22–25:

> *"Turn to me and be saved,*
> *all the ends of the earth!*
> *For I am God, and there is no other.*

---

17. "Christian Hope and a Millennium," p. 13.

18. *Systematic Theology,* 3:800–805.

> *By myself I have sworn,*
>   *from my mouth has gone forth*
>   *in righteousness*
>   *a word that shall not return:*
> *'To me every knee shall bow,*
>   *every tongue shall swear.'*
> *Only in the LORD, it shall be said of me,*
>   *are righteousness and strength;*
> *to him shall come and be ashamed,*
>   *all who were incensed against him.*
> *In the LORD all the offspring of Israel*
>   *shall triumph and glory."*

While this quotation is part of a passage that speaks of Jehovah's dealing with His chosen nation Israel, it seems to speak of a universal acceptance of Him, and hence a universal reign by Him. Hosea 2:23 also appears to indicate an extension of the covenant to those who were not then in it. The prophets certainly were not pessimistic about the future rule of the Lord.

The Psalms, particularly Psalms 47, 72, and 110, also speak repeatedly of the universality of the Messiah's rule. But Jesus quoted Psalm 110:1 as a proof of His deity (Luke 20:42–43), and Peter said it was fulfilled at Pentecost (Acts 2:34–35). Therefore it is not to be fulfilled in some cataclysmic future coming but within the present age.

Second, Jesus repeatedly said that the gospel will be universally preached and that this will take place before His second coming. For example: "And this gospel of the kingdom will be preached throughout the whole world, as a testimony to all nations; and then the end will come" (Matt. 24:14). Premillennialists see this preaching as extending to all nations, but not very effectively. It will serve as a testimony but will not result in any substantial number of conversions. The postmillennialist regards it as strange that there should be only a sort of nominal preaching, a preaching without success. What is the point of such preaching, unless it is only to condemn? Where is the power that presumably accompanies the church in its preaching? The postmillennialist sees periods of broadening religious and spiritual interest, such as the 1950s in the United States, as supporting this central contention. Even the rising interest in the supernatural demonic, although it at first may militate against the success of the gospel, may well indicate a future breakthrough not far removed in time.

Third, the great commission that Christ gave His apostles after His resurrection was to take the gospel message to every nation and every creature. This process of taking the message is to continue to the end of the age, and its purpose is to make disciples of all the nations, baptizing and instructing them (Matt. 28:19–20). This certainly does not seem to fit the premillennial characterization of this preaching as being merely a witness or testimony.

Further, this commission is distinguished by the authority possessed and conferred by the Lord who issued it.[19] Jesus said that all power or authority had been given to Him. He will never have more authority at any point in the future than He now has, for He has all there is. Hence we need not look to a future age when He will be capable of bringing in the complete reign prophesied. He is as capable of doing it now as He will be in the future. Premillennialists assert that Christ the King is absent and will do great things when He returns; postmillennialists assert, however, that according to this passage Christ *is* present and will be to the end of the age. Thus that power to conquer and reign is available to us in the present.

The postmillennialist also observes that the promised national conversion of the Jews is not to take place until "the full number of the Gentiles come in" (Rom. 11:25). This seems to suggest a completeness to the conversion of the Gentile nations.

One of the evidences that this gospel is succeeding is the improvement of the world. Not only are individuals being redeemed, but concomitantly and consequently the world is being redeemed as well. While there are setbacks within the general trend and the progress is sometimes too slow and gradual to be noticeable, the trend is for good to advance and evil to decline. Boettner sees great progress from the period before Christ to the present. Ultimately this process will be completed; before Christ returns, we shall see a Christianized world.

Prior to the coming of Christ, society was characterized by awful moral and spiritual conditions—for example, slavery, polygamy, oppression of women and children, lack of political

---

19. Boettner, *The Millennium*, p. 28.

freedom. Now, however, slavery and polygamy have virtually disappeared, social and economic conditions have reached new high levels in practically all nations, and a spirit of cooperation is found among nations to a degree that has not been true before.[20] In particular, Boettner cited the foreign aid and mutual security program of the United States. The huge amount of goods given by this enlightened and predominantly Protestant nation without expecting anything in return is evidence of a changing, improving world.[21]

Another indication of the progress of the gospel is the widespread availability and distribution of the Scriptures in the common language of the people. The growth of Christian radio programs, seminaries, Bible institutes, magazines, and other means of disseminating the gospel has also encouraged Boettner.[22]

Acknowledging that the relative growth of Christianity has been slow, Boettner blamed this on the failure of Christians in general to take seriously the command of Christ to evangelize the world.[23] It in no sense argues against the efficacy of the gospel.

Some postmillennialists, like some premillennialists, have attempted to set dates. As recently as 1919 James H. Snowden saw the First World War ending militarism forever and beginning a rapid development toward the millennium.[24] Boettner regards date-setting of any kind to be dangerous. His confidence in Christian progress is not tied to the identification of any specific events as indications of the gospel's triumph, but rather to the teaching of Scripture regarding long-range developments in the world.[25]

Great material prosperity is displayed in many ways today. As impressive as this is, however, it is and always will remain simply a by-product of the moral and spiritual progress and prosperity increasingly coming upon us.[26]

---

20. Ibid., p. 38.
21. Ibid., p. 39.
22. Ibid., pp. 39–41.
23. Ibid., p. 45.
24. *The Coming of the Lord,* pp. 268ff.
25. *The Millennium,* p. 47.
26. Ibid., p. 52.

The Nature of the Kingdom

Another significant distinguishing feature of post-millennialism is its view that the kingdom of God is a present earthly reality, not a future heavenly reality. It is here and now, and it is growing gradually. It is not something which at the moment is absent but which will be inaugurated by one major event. Instead it is arriving by degrees, almost imperceptibly.

Jesus most extensively discussed the kingdom in the parables, and particularly the parables of Matthew 13. Of the seven parables recorded in that chapter, four compare the kingdom of heaven to processes of growth.[27]

Leaven is a particularly apt illustration of the kingdom's progressive coming.[28] Leaven works its way, atom by atom, through the meal until it pervades the whole mass. Many premillennialists hold that leaven here is a type not of good and of the gospel's power, but of evil, as it is in so many other places in Scripture. The postmillennialist, however, finds this interpretation forced and far-fetched. As the leaven gradually but surely permeates the whole, so the gospel is being effectively taken throughout the world. Eventually the entirety will feel the effect of the gospel's power.

The parables of the tares and the draw-net teach that the growth of the kingdom of God will be a mixed growth.[29] When the servants examine the growing grain, they see intermingled with it, weeds ("tares"). They propose to remove them by rooting them out. The master forbids them to do this, however, because the enemy who has sown the weeds has sown them so skillfully that one can scarcely distinguish the grain from the weeds. The prohibition is to prevent some of the good from being destroyed with the evil. This parable seems to indicate that the two classes of persons are virtually indistinguishable. This is also taught in the parable of the draw-net. Good fish and bad alike are caught in the net. After the fish are sorted, the bad are cast away. Premillennialists have cited these two parables as evidence that the world is not to grow better through the preaching of the gospel, but worse. On the

---

27. Snowden, *The Coming of the Lord*, p. 72.

28. Ibid., p. 73.

29. Ibid., pp. 74–75.

contrary, insist postmillennialists, the tares are a comparatively negligible part of the total picture. We may expect to see at the end of the world a full wheat field with relatively few tares. The kingdom is not now, never has been, and never will be, free from attendant evils, but these evils are quite minor. Further, through the "biology of grace," tares may become wheat in the field. This is a transmutation that nature cannot achieve, but with God all things are possible. The parable of the tares warns against attempts to purify the church by purging it of unworthy members and suspected heresy. A trust in the grace of God relieves one from the responsibility to take such matters into one's own hands.

The growth of the kingdom is both intensive and extensive, each aspect of which is affirmed and illustrated by different parables. The parables of the sower and the mustard seed illustrate intensive growth.[30] The grain stays in its own field, and the mustard tree remains attached to its own roots. The growth of each consists in developing its own life into complete fruition. The kingdom of God grows similarly. Each one who enters the kingdom develops in grace, growing up to maturity, as Paul pointed out in Ephesians 4:13. Individual believers become, in a sense, more fully members of the kingdom of God. It is even conceivable that the kingdom might be planted in one place or in a limited group of people and, while continuing to grow, remain right there for a time.

The extensive growth of the kingdom is seen in the parable of the leaven.[31] As in all the parables of growth, the field is the world. Just as natural leaven develops from one atom or segment to the next, so the gospel leaven works its way through society from individual to individual. This was illustrated in the ministry of Jesus when Andrew brought his brother to Jesus and when Philip brought Nathanael. What began then has continued to the present time. What is true of the gospel's spread from individual to individual is true of its spread through society's institutions and activities—physical environment, houses, education, politics, national and international affairs. In this way the whole mass of humanity shall be imbued with and governed by Christian principles and spirit.

30. Ibid., p. 76.
31. Ibid., pp. 76–77.

This growth, because it is slow, may require a long period of time.[32] It is not a sudden explosion. As the growth of a tree cannot be noticed in a day, nor the movement of a clock's hour hand observed in a second, so the growth of the kingdom may be virtually imperceptible, particularly in its initial stages. While postmillennialists concede that the kingdom has made comparatively small progress in the world, they believe that progress will accelerate. As a snowball grows slowly when small but more rapidly as its surface increases, so does the kingdom. The growth, in the language of mathematics, is exponential. As each person who enters the kingdom wins another, there will be a great crescendo. One may look at the present state of the kingdom and ask, "If this is proportionately how far it has come in this length of time, how long will it take for it to be completely established?" This is misleading, however, for the kingdom is still in an early phase of its development.

The postmillennialist is not in a hurry. God does not rush matters. Once we believed that the earth is only a few thousand years old and that man is even younger. Now, however, we have learned from geology and anthropology that these figures must be revised sharply upward.[33] Just as God took millions and perhaps billions of years to prepare the earth for human habitation, so He will take a long time to complete His redemptive plan.

This gradual growth, however, is also attended by crises.[34] Even in nature, where growth processes are usually steady, there are crises and cataclysmic developments. A plant may develop for years and then suddenly burst into bloom. The ripening of grain for harvest is a type of crisis, as are the metamorphoses of insects.

It is therefore in accord with natural laws of development for the gradual processes to be marked by dramatic or cataclysmic events. This is apparent in the history of God's dealings with His people. The call of Abraham, the exodus, the captivity, the return from exile, the coming of Christ, the death and resurrection of Christ, Pentecost, and the first and second general councils at Jerusalem (Acts 11 and 15) were obviously epochal events. So were the

---

32. Ibid., p. 78.

33. Ibid., p. 79.

34. Ibid., pp. 81–84.

fall of Jerusalem, the conversion of the Roman empire, and the Reformation. Some postmillennialists viewed the First World War in the same light, seeing it as the means by which military despotism would be rooted out.[35]

The final great catastrophe in this series will be the second coming of the Lord. Yet this is not, as with the premillennialist, so much a culminating step in the process, accomplishing the final and complete introduction of the kingdom, as it is an announcement of the kingdom. Christ will return after the great commission has been fulfilled and all nations have been discipled and baptized.

The Nature of the Millennium

For the postmillennialist the thousand years of Revelation 20 are symbolic in nature. While it is somewhat questionable whether Warfield was postmillennial or amillennial, his interpretation of the thousand years has been cited with approval by Boettner, an avowed postmillennialist.[36] Boettner feels that the meaning of *millennium* is qualitative rather than quantitative. One interpretation is that the first resurrection refers to the reanimating of the spirit of those who were martyred in the early history of the church.[37] Another view is that the first resurrection refers to the ascension to heaven of these martyrs, who now reign with Christ in what is sometimes termed the "intermediate state."[38] The point is that the doctrine of the millennium is based not upon Revelation 20 but upon other portions of Scripture. The word *millennium* probably ought always to be enclosed in quotation marks. There will be a long period of time, indefinite in length, when the Lord will reign over the earth. This reign will be progressively established, and because of this gradual inception, the exact length of the period will be difficult to measure or calculate.

Postmillennialism shares many features with either premillennialism or amillennialism or both. Perhaps its most distinc-

---

35. Ibid., pp. 268–70.
36. *The Millennium,* p. 64.
37. Snowden, *The Coming of the Lord,* pp. 178–79.
38. Ibid., pp. 181–84.

tive feature is its optimism. Premillennialists believe that spiritual conditions will worsen and unbelief increase, and amillennialists tend to think the same way. Postmillennialists believe that through the preaching of the gospel, the world will be Christianized, and with that will come peace and other phenomena of the kingdom of God.

Evaluation of Postmillennialism

Having seen something of the history of postmillennialism and its principal tenets, we must now evaluate it. What are its strengths and its weaknesses?

Positive Aspects

Beginning with the positive side, we note that post-millennialism has correctly given attention to a genuinely Biblical theme—the present dimension of the kingdom of God. Jesus said that the kingdom was near, that it was among men, and He spoke of men entering the kingdom. In all of this He certainly appeared to say that this kingdom was not purely a future reality. The King is absent in one sense, but in another sense he is definitely present (Matt. 28:19–20). Knowing that our Lord and King is present and that His resources are available to us now, our life style should be characterized by confidence, optimism, and aggressiveness.

Postmillennialism has also rightly encouraged an activism on the part of believers. If the kingdom is present, we can do something to extend it. In this way the doctrine of Christianity can support its ethic. The parables of Jesus in particular show the kingdom to be growing by degrees, not merely springing up full blown in a distant ἔσχατον. Understanding that the kingdom can and does grow little by little helps us see our part in bringing that kingdom by spreading the gospel to other men and by promoting Christian ways of living. This is commanded in Scripture, and the postmillennial description of the kingdom supports this command.

Postmillennialism also is Biblical in promoting a spirit of optimism and combating the sort of pessimism to which some Christians have allowed themselves to fall victim. Jesus did promise power to those who would bear the gospel (Acts 1:8). He spoke of the kingdom permeating the whole world. The Biblical descriptions

70

of the apostasy and wickedness which will characterize the end times have made some Christians fatalistic. Conditions will become worse and worse, they say, and we can do nothing to alter them. This kind of thinking makes the church less effective than it would otherwise be, and evil more pervasive. Because confidence and expectation are so important to success, postmillennialism contributes to the fulfillment of what is predicted.

Further, postmillennialism recognizes that the kingdom of God is broader than the church. Wherever the will of God is done, there the reign of God is present, even if only partially or fragmentarily. This may be true even when the one performing the act is not aware that he is doing God's will. He may not be consciously committed to God. This means that God may accomplish His will at least in part through non-Christian persons, agencies, nations, and ideologies. If He employed Babylonia and Assyria in Biblical times, He can do something similar in our day. This means that the Christian can and should work constructively with any person or agent who is acting with some part or aspect of God's kingdom. It also means that the kingdom is, to a large extent, an ethical kingdom.

Negative Aspects

On the other hand, postmillennialism has certain shortcomings. One is its optimism concerning the conversion of the world, which seems somewhat unrealistic in the light of recent world developments. The percentage of Christians in the world is not increasing. In fact, a lower percentage of the world's population is even nominally Christian than was the case ten, thirty, or fifty years ago. Even the opportunities for propagating the gospel seem to be fading. Mainland China has been closed to missionaries for a quarter century—although recent political developments offer some hope for change—and some sections of India are similarly closed. The prospects for worldwide conversion seem poor. The same is true of the structures of society. The hope that the First World War would end war proved false. The League of Nations was unsuccessful, and the United Nations has been only partially successful. While technological progress is undeniable, there has not been comparable social and ethical progress.

71

This criticism, it must be admitted, may have to be qualified eventually. Perhaps sometime beyond the foreseeable future present trends will be reversed. For the postmillennial hope to materialize, however, a rather radical reversal of current trends would be required.

Perhaps more damaging to postmillennialism is its apparent neglect of Scripture passages (e.g., Matt. 24:9–14) that portray spiritual and moral conditions as worsening in the end times. It appears that postmillennialism has based its doctrine on very carefully selected Scripture passages.

Even in the passages that postmillennialists discuss, some selectivity seems to be at work. For example, in the parable of the tares and the grain, there is no indication that the tares are ever transmuted into good grain; at the end they have to be rooted out and destroyed. Because it does not fit their position, postmillennialists largely ignore this dimension of the account.

There is also some artificiality in the postmillennialists' treatment of the two resurrections and the millennium in Revelation 20. This will be shown more clearly when we evaluate amillennialism; it will suffice now to note that postmillennialists brush aside the fact that the descriptions of the two resurrections are very similar.

Finally, postmillennialists have had some difficulty maintaining a genuine supernaturalism. As their view of the kingdom became more diffuse, regarding it as the reign of God everywhere, some failed to discriminate between good and evil. For example, some saw the kingdom being fulfilled even through Nazism. The Biblical antithesis between the good and holy kingdom of God, which will be present completely only when Christ returns personally, and the kingdom of evil, with which God's kingdom is always in conflict in this life, was diminished.

Chapter 4

Amillennialism

The eschatological system referred to as amillennialism, while it is in some ways the clearest and simplest of the several systems, presents special difficulties. This view can be briefly stated: there will be no earthly, thousand-year reign of Christ. Yet there are several obstacles to a clear understanding of it.

First, amillennialism has frequently been stated in a primarily negative fashion, and consequently its positive features have not always emerged clearly. Because many of the recent presentations of amillennialism have been primarily criticisms of premillennialism, its positive dimensions have been somewhat distorted.

Further, so many explanations of and arguments for amillennialism have been offered that it tends to be a bit confusing, to say the least. At times one almost wonders if one is dealing with subtypes of a single basic view or with different views.

Finally, amillennialism has often been difficult to distinguish from postmillennialism. Such men as Augustine (354–430), John Calvin (1509–1564), and Benjamin B. Warfield (1851–1921) have been claimed by both groups. Unless a man addresses the specific issues that separate the two positions, he may not clearly enunciate his stand. This has led to confusion. Most amillennialists have tended to distinguish their position from premillennialism rather than from postmillennialism, and most have shown considerable sympathy for postmillennialism. Many amillennialists, indeed, are former postmillennialists. This has further blurred the differences between the two views.

Overview of Amillennialism

In examining the general features of amillennialism, we might best proceed by noting those tenets it holds in common with post-millennialism. The first is that the second coming of Christ will inaugurate the final age and the final state for both believers and unbelievers. This means that the second coming will be followed immediately by the general resurrection, the judgment of all men, and the consignment of all to their ultimate, future states. There will be no transitional period, no earthly, personal reign of Christ, no millennium. These events will follow in rapid sequence, with no appreciable intervening period of time.

The second feature (shared at least with most postmillennialists) is that the one thousand years of Revelation 20 are symbolical rather than literal. Another way of putting this is to say that the reference to one thousand years is atemporal. The postmillennialist believes in an earthly reign of Christ, but with Christ absent instead of present. This belief, however, is not based on Revelation 20; indeed, this passage is regarded as irrelevant to the issue.

Further, the two resurrections of Revelation 20 do not, as the premillennialist contends, require an intervening millennium. Amillennialists have agreed that the two resurrections are not both physical. Some amillennialists, however, regard the first resurrection as spiritual and the second as physical; others regard both resurrections as spiritual.

Finally, Old Testament prophecies are less literal than most premillennialists consider them. These prophecies will not be fulfilled in a thousand-year, earthly period; they tend rather to be fulfilled within the history of the church, or in some cases in the "new earth."[1]

There are also some points of congruency between amillennialism and premillennialism. The first is a pessimistic outlook. The amillennialist does not anticipate a worldwide growth of righteousness that will extend to every area of society.[2] Amillennialists vary in their estimates of how successfully the gospel will be preached. Some grant the possibility of worldwide conversions, in which case

---

1. W. J. Grier, "Christian Hope and the Millennium," p. 19.
2. Ibid.

all will confess Christ as Lord and we will be able to say that Christ's reign is present, His kingdom has come. Many amillennialists, however, doubt that evangelization will be so successful. The number who believe and are saved will thus be only a small segment or remnant of the world population. While amillennialists do not relish this prospect, they believe it is consistent with the teaching of Scripture and the recent course of world events. Thus, an amillennialist may be just as certain as the typical premillennialist that the faith of many will grow cold.

Further, the amillennialist believes in the imminence of Christ's second coming. While this term has many different shades of meaning, it does mean, in general, that the Lord could return virtually at any time. For the postmillennialist, the Lord will not return until the gospel has been spread worldwide and the world has enjoyed a period of peace. The amillennialist and premillennialist, however, do not believe that these phenomena will precede the Lord's coming. Thus, with no major events of long duration yet to be fulfilled, the Lord could come at any time. It should be noted, however, that while this tenet is shared by amillennialists and premillennialists, it does not produce the same mood or tone in the typical amillennialist that it often does in the premillennialist. Thus, the amillennialist seldom bemoans the deterioration of world conditions or condemns the prevalent culture. He has noticeably less preoccupation with the details and sequence of the last things and less curiosity about "signs of the times." Indeed, the whole subject of eschatology seems to receive less attention from amillennial theologians than from premillennial theologians, particularly those who are dispensational. Genuine amillennialism has an ethos all its own.

History of Amillennialism

Some have found amillennial elements very early in the history of the church. Diedrich H. Kromminga, a premillennialist, discerned in the Epistle of Barnabas "a very early amillennial type of eschatology,"[3] and the Epistle of Barnabas is one of the earliest Christian writings outside the Bible itself. Kromminga's contention,

---

3. *The Millennium in the Church: Studies in the History of Christian Chiliasm,* p. 40.

however, is disputed by other students of church history. Nonetheless, amillennialism has no doubt been present, in a form not always differentiated from postmillennialism, during long periods of church history.

Even if there was no thoroughgoing amillennialism in the earliest centuries of the church, at least amillennial elements probably were present. Augustine, however, was the one who systematized and developed the approach. Because he was in the vanguard in a number of areas of thought, one finds "confused" in his writings emphases that later theologians clearly distinguished. Thus, both amillennialists and postmillennialists can with some justification claim him for their positions. The most significant point (for our purposes) that Augustine made is that the millennium is not primarily temporal or chronological. Its significance is rather in what it symbolizes. This tradition was carried on through the church in both Catholic and Protestant varieties. It is likely that what we now call amillennialism and postmillennialism were found together until the nineteenth century, when postmillennialism was first developed in thoroughgoing fashion.

With the decline of postmillennialism during the twentieth century, rather large numbers of former postmillennialists found it necessary to adjust their eschatology. Because premillennialism represented too sharp a break, the majority opted for amillennialism. The recent rise in the popularity of amillennialism can therefore be related to the events precipitating the crisis for postmillennialism. For some, it was clearly an exchange of tenets. For others, it was simply adopting a position on an issue on which they had taken no position previously. In any event, the alternatives have narrowed somewhat, so that in practice the choice is between amillennialism and premillennialism. Conservatives in the historic Reformed groups—denominations like the Reformed Church of America and the Christian Reformed Church, as well as many Presbyterian ones—are primarily amillennial.

Tenets of Amillennialism

The Two Resurrections

A significant element of amillennialism is its treatment of the two resurrections referred to in Revelation 20:4–5: "They came to life [the first resurrection], and reigned with Christ a thousand years. The rest of the dead did not come to life until the thousand years were ended [the second resurrection]." The first resurrection, say amillennialists, is spiritual, the second is either bodily-physical or spiritual. Most amillennialists consider the second resurrection to be physical, and writers like Floyd E. Hamilton have presented the arguments for this position. A more recent presentation of this position appeared in a 1960 article by Ray Summers.

Summers emphasized the importance of basing the interpretation of Revelation 20 upon that of the entire Book of Revelation.[4] In other words, chapter 20 must be seen in the wider context of the entire book. One must begin by asking, "What did the book's message mean to those to whom it was originally addressed?" Summers believes the book was written in the last decade of the first Christian century to Christians in Asia Minor who were undergoing severe persecution at the hands of a Roman government that hoped to destroy Christianity. The purpose of the book was to assure God's people that Christ will triumph over all opposition.[5]

Satan was attempting to deceive believers into worshiping the emperor rather than Christ. The binding of Satan referred to in Revelation 20:1–3 is to incapacitate him for effectively continuing this work. The one thousand years symbolizes the completeness of this binding and restraint.[6]

This same symbol of one thousand years is used to convey the idea of the complete triumph of the martyrs who have been objects of Satan's wrath.[7] In Revelation 6:9–11 these martyred souls are under the altar, questioning how long it will be until God intervenes to halt the success of the wicked one. In Revelation 20:4–5 they are on thrones with Christ for a thousand years. The description of them makes it almost undeniable that they are the ones who have given their lives rather than succumbed to the demands of the emperor.

---

4. "Revelation 20: An Interpretation," p. 176. For more complete statements by Summers, see *Worthy Is the Lamb: An Interpretation of Revelation* and *The Life Beyond*.

5. "Revelation 20," p. 176.

6. Ibid., p. 179.

7. Ibid., p. 180.

On this basis, then, the first resurrection symbolizes the victory of the martyrs. Particularly significant is the statement: "Blessed and holy is he who shares in the first resurrection! Over such the second death has no power. . . ." (20:6). This suggests that the second death, customarily understood by eschatologists of all millennial persuasions to be a spiritual death, corresponds to the first resurrection. This implies that the first resurrection similarly is spiritual. There is also a reference to a second resurrection ("The rest of the dead did not come to life until . . .", 20:5), although it is not explicitly denominated the second resurrection. While not mentioned, there is implied a first death, which would be physical. To this corresponds the second resurrection, which would then also be physical. Summers believes this idea was presented by way of *chiasmos*, a Greek literary and poetic device according to which the four elements of a proposition are presented in diagonal fashion. He diagrammed the form thus:[8]

"First resurrection" = a symbol of the martyrs' triumph

"Second resurrection" ("coming to life," 20:5) = the general, physical resurrection taught in the New Testament

"First death" (not mentioned but implied) = physical death

"Second death" = a symbol of eternal punishment in separation from the blessings of God

This interpretation has been presented in a variety of ways by other authors. W. J. Grier has also maintained that those participating in the first resurrection (20:6) are the blessed dead. He noted that the expression "risen with Christ" is used to describe Christians in several New Testament passages (Rom. 6:1–11; Eph. 2:1–10; Col. 3:1–4).[9] Thus there is a good basis for interpreting the "first resurrection" in Revelation 20:6 as spiritual rather than physical.

Premillennialists have usually centered their criticism of this amillennial interpretation of the two resurrections on the fact that

---

8. Ibid., p. 182.
9. "Christian Hope," p. 19.

the same Greek word is used of both resurrections: "They came to life (ἔζησαν), and reigned with Christ a thousand years. The rest of the dead did not come to life (ἔζησαν) until the thousand years were ended." There is, premillennialists argue, no justifiable basis for making these two resurrections different in kind. If one is physical, the other must be also. Nothing in the context indicates otherwise.

Taking this criticism seriously, James A. Hughes has assayed an entirely different treatment of the passage. Hughes acknowledged the force of the argument that ἔζησαν must be used in the same sense in both occurrences. He commended the premillennialists for their exegetical accuracy in this matter and for their consistency in interpreting both as bodily resurrections.[10] Recognizing the validity of this logic, he refused to interpret the ἔζησαν of verse 4 as a spiritual resurrection and the same verb in verse 5 as a physical resurrection. This view, he wrote, "is hardly tenable." This would seem to leave him impaled upon the horns of a dilemma, but he found still another option: make both verbs apply to a spiritual resurrection. His argument proceeds in three steps: (1) the first ἔζησαν is spiritual, not physical and bodily; (2) the first and second resurrections are parallel; and (3) the second resurrection is also spiritual.

Hughes began his argument by noting that those involved in the first resurrection are pictured as disembodied souls sitting on judgment-thrones and reigning, with judging being part of reigning. He is aware that the term ψυχή can (and frequently does) designate the whole person rather than merely a part, which fact Charles L. Feinberg cited in his defense of premillennialism and refutation of amillennialism. Hughes granted this fact but maintained that ψυχή rarely designates the whole person when it is followed, as it is here, by the genitive of the noun. In a detailed footnote he examined several similar usages of the expression in the New Testament and concluded that here, as in Revelation 6:9, "These expressions clearly refer to disembodied souls."[11] While it is not completely clear whether Revelation 20:4 contains three groups or one, Hughes believes that it contains basically one, with the expression

10. "Revelation 20:4–6 and the Question of the Millennium," p. 300.
11. Ibid., p. 288.

"the souls of those who had been beheaded for their testimony to Jesus" uniting what precedes with what follows. Since judgment is part of reigning, those who sit on judgment-thrones are the same disembodied souls who reign with Christ for a thousand years.

This presents immediate difficulties for the view that John is describing a bodily or physical resurrection. One is that souls, unlike bodies, cannot die and be resurrected.

Another difficulty for the premillennialist interpretation is the fact that ἔζησαν is in the aorist tense. In its most common usage the aorist of this verb would simply be rendered, "they lived." It is true that a less common usage, the "ingressive aorist," would be rendered, "they began to live" or "they came to life." If ἔζησαν is ingressive, however, so is the verb translated "reigned," because it too is aorist and it is parallel to ἔζησαν. Thus if they "came to life," they also "began to reign." Further, since the reigning is for a thousand years, so is the living.[12] We would then have to say, in effect, "they came to life a thousand years, and they began to reign a thousand years," which at the very least would require a very slow resurrection and a very slow inception of their reign. Hence, Hughes concluded that the only plausible rendering of ἔζησαν is "they lived," the aorist being constative, or historical.

To further support this contention, Hughes suggested that in only two places in the New Testament can the aorist indicative of ζάω be construed as an ingressive aorist, and both refer to the resurrection of Christ. In Revelation 2:8 Christ described Himself as the one "who became dead (ἐγένετο νεκρὸς) and came to life (ἔζησεν)." Romans 14:9, then, may be rendered: "For to this end Christ became dead (ἀπέθανεν, from ἀποθνήσκω) and came to life (ἔζησεν)." (Although Hughes did not call attention to it, the verb ἀποθνήσκω in the aorist tense contains an ingressive element within it, for it means "to die," not "to be dead"). Further, Hughes noted, it is not the same to say that someone "became dead and came to life" and to say that someone saw the souls of those who had been beheaded and who came to life. The proper translation, therefore, is "they lived."

There is a problem for Hughes's view, however.[13] The references in Revelation 20:4 to "coming to life" (RSV) or "living"

---

12. Ibid., p. 290.   13. Ibid., pp. 292–93.

(KJV) are specifically referred to in verse 5 as "the first resurrection." Is it possible to speak of disembodied souls being raised? Hughes stated that the term *resurrection* is not confined in Scripture to the body. One example occurs in Luke 20, the discussion of the woman who had been married successively to seven brothers. Some Sadducees asked Jesus, Whose wife will she be "in the resurrection"? Both the question and Jesus' answer indicate that "the resurrection" here means "the next life" or "the next world." Jesus' proof that the dead are raised is that Moses referred to the Lord as the God of Abraham, Isaac, and Jacob, all of whom had died. Because God is not the God of the dead but of the living, the patriarchs must have been raised. Since their bodies had not yet been raised, however, "the resurrection" must in this passage be synonymous with "the next life" or "heaven."[14]

A second example cited by Hughes is I Corinthians 15.[15] This has generally been interpreted as saying that the bodily resurrection of believers is assured because Christ's body was resurrected. Hughes reasoned differently. Paul seems to have been saying that if Christ was not raised from the dead, then those who have died in Christ have perished (i.e., they are not alive) and we have hope only in this life. But Christ *was* raised from the dead. Therefore, those who have died in Him have not perished (i.e., they are alive; they have obtained that world; they have been "raised from the dead"). Here, Hughes argued, it is evident that *resurrection* does not refer to bodily resurrection; it speaks of being alive, of the survival of the soul, or of spiritual resurrection. It affirms that death does not end it all. Those who have died *have been* raised from the dead. Hughes recognized that in this interpretation of I Corinthians 15 he was parting company with Charles Hodge and Calvin, leading representatives of the Reformed tradition of which he is part. He nonetheless was emphatic in support of his interpretation.

Hughes's final example is Hebrews 11:35,[16] which he translated: "Women received their dead raised to life again: and others were tortured, not accepting deliverance; that they might obtain a

---

14. Ibid., pp. 293–94.
15. Ibid., pp. 295–98.
16. Ibid., p. 298.

better resurrection." Here he found a contrast between being raised to life and obtaining a "better resurrection," which he interpreted to be a spiritual resurrection, or immortality.

When Revelation 20 is examined closely against this background, definite conclusions follow. The term *first resurrection* implies a *second resurrection,* and the term *second death* implies a *first death;* yet the terms *second resurrection* and *first death* are missing, a fact that Hughes regarded as significant. There is an emphasis here upon the difference between two groups. Verse 4b says, "they lived and reigned with Christ a thousand years," while 5a says, "but the rest of the dead lived not again until the thousand years were finished" (KJV). One group *lived* during the thousand years and the other group *did not,* though both groups were physically dead. There are the "living" dead, who have part in the first resurrection and over whom the second death has no power, and the "dead" dead, who have no part in the first resurrection and over whom the second death does have power. The second death has power over "the rest of the dead" with respect to their souls, just as the former group are souls (v. 4). Therefore, the first death must be physical and the second resurrection spiritual, pertaining to the just and unjust alike.[17]

Hughes is aware of the standard objection to his view. Verse 5a says that "the rest of the dead lived not again until the thousand years were finished." Does this not indicate that after the thousand years "the rest of the dead"—those who were not resurrected at the beginning of the thousand years—will be resurrected bodily? Hughes said no. He first observed that the verb and negative particle are οὐκ ἔζησαν ("they did not live") rather than οὐκ ἀνέζησαν ("they did not live again"). Second, verse 5a says that the rest of the dead did not live "until" (ἄχρι) the thousand years were finished, which is equivalent to saying that the rest of the dead did not live *during* the thousand years. Those over whom the second death has power are never released from its power. "The rest of the dead" will not live until the thousand years are finished, nor will they live thereafter. Here is Hughes's unique exegetical contribution: the word ἄχρι ("until") does not of itself imply that a change occurs after the point to which it refers. This is apparent, for

---

17. Ibid., pp. 299–300.

example, in Romans 5:13a: "For until (ἄχρι) the law sin was in the world" (KJV). Certainly sin was in the world both up until the coming of the Mosaic law and after its coming; sin is obviously still very much in the world.[18]

To summarize Hughes's view: The two resurrections are similar in nature. The first resurrection is spiritual, the ascension of the soul to heaven. The second resurrection is also spiritual, but it is virtually hypothetical in nature. The passage in its entirety describes disembodied souls in the intermediate state, saying nothing about bodily resurrection.

The Nature of the Millennium

Another important tenet of amillennialism is its interpretation of the thousand years in Revelation 20. Verse 2 speaks of Satan being bound for a thousand years, and verse 4 of those who have been beheaded for their testimony to Jesus, reigning with Him for a thousand years. The interpretation of these two references requires first that we see the nature of the entire book and the place of this portion within it.

The amillennialist generally sees Revelation as composed of several sections (usually seven), each of which recapitulates the events of the same period rather than describing the events of successive periods. Each deals with the same era—the period between Christ's first and second comings—picking up earlier themes, elaborating and developing them further. Revelation 20, then, does not speak of far-removed, future events, and the meaning of the thousand years is to be found in some past and/or present fact.[19]

Further, and even more generally, the passage must be understood within the broad context of the book as a whole. One must remember that Revelation is a very symbolic and figurative book. Not even premillennialists press all of its images for literal meanings. If one would, the result would be ludicrous. When chapter 20 speaks of the binding of Satan, for example, certainly no one thinks this will be done with a literal chain of metal. Few would see the bowls, seals, and trumpets as literal. Therefore, it seems

---

18. Ibid., pp. 301–2.

19. Floyd E. Hamilton, *The Basis of Millennial Faith,* pp. 130–31.

reasonable to conclude that the number one thousand might not be literal, either. In addition, the fact that nowhere else in Scripture is there an explicit reference to such a period of earthly reign calls into question the importance that premillennialists have attached to this doctrine.

If the number one thousand is symbolic, what does it symbolize? Many theologians have followed the suggestion of Warfield, who has been claimed by both amillennialists and postmillennialists but whose word on this matter has seemed almost determinative: "The sacred number seven in combination with the equally sacred number three forms the number of holy perfection, ten, and when this ten is cubed into a thousand the seer has said all he could say to convey to our minds the idea of absolute completeness."[20] One might question why, in attempting to discern the meaning of the number ten, we should investigate the meaning of seven and three instead of, say, six and four, but many amillennialists regard Warfield's approach as correct.

This completeness or perfection, then, is applied to both references to "a thousand years." In verse 2, it is seen as the totality of Christ's triumph over Satan and his forces of evil.[21] In verse 4, on the other hand, it is seen as the completeness of the present glory and bliss of the redeemed in heaven.

The Interpretation of Prophecy

We should also note that at base the amillennialist approaches the interpretation of prophecy differently from the premillennialist. The amillennialist tends to expect no literal fulfillment of prophecy at some future time. Many of the prophecies he considers either to have been fulfilled relatively soon after the prophecy itself or, as in the case of the martyrs who reign with Christ for a thousand years, to describe ongoing conditions. (The passage concerning the reigning martyrs is understood "reiteratively"—it finds its fulfillment constantly in the intermediate state of believers.) In this way the amillennialist sidesteps the premillennial argument that there are numerous prophecies yet to be

---

20. "The Millennium and the Apocalypse," p. 654.
21. Grier, "Christian Hope," p. 19.

fulfilled and that these require a millennium. This is the source of the different tone or ethos of the thought and writings of amillennialists on the one hand and of premillennialists on the other. Premillennialists are often "searching the Scriptures" and studying current events, attempting to align the two to discover how near the end might be. Generally speaking, amillennialists do not possess nearly as intensive a prophetic interest.

Evaluation of Amillennialism

In the amillennial system we have much that is commendable and cogent, as well as points of weakness and even of inconsistency.

Positive Aspects

On the positive side, amillennialism recognizes that Biblical prophecy and eschatology utilize a great deal of symbolism and handles it accordingly. Some millennialists have dealt with the images in eschatological passages in too straightforward a fashion, though few expositors have carried out this principle consistently. Some passages rather obviously represent something beyond their immediate and literal meaning. The amillennialist, by and large, has attempted to take seriously the nature of Biblical literature and has asked what was being conveyed within that cultural setting, realizing that symbolism may be present and operative even when it is not obvious. At its best, amillennialism has also attempted to determine the proper meaning of the symbols by studying the culture rather than by assigning a meaning arbitrarily.

Second, amillennialism has attempted to do serious exegesis of the relevant Biblical passage, Revelation 20. In part this was a response to the question of the premillennialists, What does the passage mean if it does not teach an earthly millennium? From the perspective of one who believes that the Bible is the supreme authority for Christian belief and practice, this scrutiny of Scripture is highly commendable. The investigation conducted by Hughes is a thorough attempt to get at the original meaning of this passage and to explicate that meaning accurately. The detail and the openness to a variety of possibilities are in the best tradition of Biblical scholarship.

It appears as well that amillennialism has a realistic philosophy of history. Its view of what is to come and where history is going fits well with recent developments and discernible trends. The amillennial view allows for either a deterioration or an improvement of conditions, teaching neither that the entire world will be converted prior to Christ's return nor that world conditions will inevitably grow worse.

Negative Aspects

When we consider the specific tenets of and arguments for amillennialism, however, we find some difficulties. One major cluster concerns the exegesis of Revelation 20.

The conventional amillennial interpretation is that there are two different types of resurrection, a spiritual and a physical resurrection, respectively. Yet, upon close examination, one wonders whether this creates a distinction where none exists. Even Hughes recognizes and acknowledges this difficulty, and offers a different interpretation for this passage. The same verb, ἔζησαν, is used of both resurrections, and there is no apparent contextual basis for discriminating between the two.

Verse 5 poses a particular problem for this interpretation. After affirming that the martyrs live and reign with Christ for a thousand years, the passage says, "The rest (οἱ λοιποί) of the dead did not come to life until the thousand years were ended." Although the passage certainly can be construed otherwise, it seems to imply that those who participate in the first resurrection do not participate in the second, for the contrast is between those raised at the beginning of the millennium and those raised at the end. The "coming to life" is, again, described similarly. Presumably those who are alive at the beginning are still alive at the end. If this is the case and if these are to be treated as two *different types* of resurrection, then the conclusion seems to follow that those who are spiritually resurrected, or born again, are not physically resurrected. But this would scarcely fit the doctrine of amillennialism! Some will contend that this imports a meaning that is not present. The grammatical purpose of οἱ λοιποί, however, seems to be to distinguish between the two groups. It should be noted that the second resurrection is not specifically identified or named, and certainly there is no suggestion that the martyrs would participate in it in the same way in which they come to life and reign as a result of the first resurrection. To be sure, the argument from silence is not a strong one. The silence, however, is found just where we should find some positive evidence.

The position argued by Hughes is, as we noted, quite different from that of Summers. Taking into account the force of objections such as those noted above, it is in many ways a fresh, original treatment of familiar data. Yet when the several detailed links of the argument are examined, difficulty is exposed.

As we noted, Hughes acknowledged that the two resurrections must be of the same class, making *both* resurrections spiritual. The evidence he adduced for this crucial assertion deserves special scrutiny.

He contended that if the first verb, ἔζησαν ("they lived"), in verse 4 is an ingressive aorist, then the second verb, ἐβασίλευσαν ("they reigned") must be the same. Thus, if one translates the first, "they came to life," he must translate the second, "they began to reign." Since this action covers a thousand years, the result is clearly ludicrous. The alternative, which would appear preferable, is to translate neither verb as an ingressive aorist: "they lived and they reigned with Christ a thousand years."

The question, however, is why both verbs must be treated the same. A. T. Robertson, whose *Grammar of the Greek New Testament in the Light of Historical Research* has long been regarded a standard authority, wrote: "A good example is ἔζησαν καὶ ἐβασίλευσαν μετὰ τοῦ Χριστοῦ χίλια ἔτη (Rev. 20:4). Here ἔζησαν is probably ingressive, though ζήσωμαν is constative in I Thess. 5:10, but ἐβασίλευσαν is clearly constative."[22] Hughes was aware of this reference and even cited it in a footnote. Yet he rejected it with only the explanation, "But this breaks the connection between ἔζησαν and ἐβασίλευσαν, and it removes ἔζησαν from any connection with the phrase χίλια ἔτη." But why should ἔζησαν be connected with the phrase χίλια ἔτη? It would seem that Hughes assumed the position he was trying to support by argument—a classic case of begging the question! Hughes should offer more substantial evidence than this, especially in the face of an authority of Robertson's stature. Hughes affirmed that the concepts of

---

22. P. 833.

judging and reigning appear to be united by the expression "the souls of them that were beheaded for the witness." He extended this to say that these souls both lived and reigned for a thousand years, but he failed to support this. It is at this point that he introduced the footnote citing Robertson.

Hughes also argued on the basis of comparative usage. He said that only in two places in the New Testament can the aorist indicative of ζάω be properly construed as ingressive. Apart from the inherent weakness of arguments based on comparative usage, Hughes neglected to explain that the aorist indicative of ζάω appears in the New Testament a total of only eight times. He concedes that two of these times it is ingressive, so the statistics in his favor are hardly impressive.

A further crucial step in his argument is that the term *resurrection* in the New Testament can mean something other than physical resuscitation. But in the examples he cited, he did not establish unequivocally that the "resurrection" involved is spiritual rather than physical. For example, his contention that in Luke 20:35 Jesus equated "to obtain that world" with "the resurrection from the dead" (KJV), is highly disputable. Hughes suggested that nothing in the context indicates that Jesus was talking about a bodily resurrection. In fact, the point was raised by the Sadducees (who denied a bodily resurrection), and Jesus' response to them was evidently intended to refute their particular heresy. It is likely that this is how Jesus' hearers understood His words. Another problem for Hughes is the lack of any clear criteria for determining when a reference to resurrection is physical and when it is spiritual. In the absence of such criteria, it may be that all references to resurrection in the Bible are spiritual. If this is the case, Hughes may have undercut the doctrine of future bodily resurrection, something he presumably does not want to do.

One further difficulty is Hughes's suggestion that "the rest of the dead," who do not live until the end of the thousand years, do not live then either. He believes that the statement, "the rest of the dead did not live until the thousand years were finished," is equivalent to saying, "the second death had power on the rest of the dead during the thousand years," to which he added, "and those on whom the second death has power are never released from its power." This latter statement is of course true if the second death is referring to spiritual death. What needs to be established, however, is that "not living" (v. 5) refers to the second death, not to the first. It is true that the second death is said to have no power over those who share in the first resurrection, but it is possible that the first death has no such power either. If it does not, then we could take the statement, "the rest of the dead did not live until the thousand years were finished," in the more natural sense that "the rest of the dead did live after the thousand years."

Chapter 5

Premillennialism

In premillennialism we have a rather popular view, particularly in evangelical or conservative circles. In some ways this view is clear, definite, simple, and straightforward. The silhouette of its major features is readily discerned. Yet, because there are two distinct varieties of premillennialism, it is sometimes difficult to determine what is generic premillennialism and what are specific features of the two subtypes. In later chapters these two varieties will be expounded in some detail. At this point, however, it will suffice to note the general features of premillennialism and then to note briefly the points of divergence.

Overview of Premillennialism

The first major feature of the premillennial system is an earthly reign of Christ that is established by His second coming. In common with postmillennialism, premillennialism asserts that there will be a period in which the will of God is done on earth, a period in which Christ's reign is an actuality among men.[1] This reign means that there will be complete peace, righteousness, and justice among men. Some premillennialists would make this a literal period of exactly one thousand years. Others would be less literal, making it simply an extended period of time. The essential point, however, is that this reign will be on earth and Jesus Christ will be

1. George E. Ladd, "The Revelation of Christ's Glory," p. 14; John F. Walvoord, "Dispensational Premillennialism," p. 11.

bodily present. According to postmillennialism, the kingdom of God will be on earth, but Christ will not have returned bodily.

Further, this earthly millennium will not come into reality through a gradual process of progressive growth or development. Rather, it will be dramatically or cataclysmically inaugurated by the second coming. While the millennium expected by post-millennialists may begin so gradually that its beginning will be virtually imperceptible, there will be no doubt about the beginning of the millennium as premillennialists envision it. The return of Christ will be similar to His departure—dramatic and external, readily observable by anyone, and consequently unmistakable.[2]

Nor will the millennium be merely an extension and perfection of trends already present on earth. It will not be brought into being by human engineering or social improvement. In fact it will be preceded by a deterioration, not an improvement, of spiritual, if not also social, conditions.[3] Premillennialists apply Christ's statement in Matthew 24:12 about men's faith growing cold to the period of time immediately before the second coming. Conditions will be transformed supernaturally, with God using His own power rather than human means to achieve His ends.

Premillennialists believe that a "great tribulation" will immediately precede the millennium, and that this will actually heighten the effects of the millennium. This will be a time of intense anguish, truly unlike anything previously occurring upon the earth. It may well involve cosmic phenomena, persecution, and great suffering. Premillennialists differ as to whether the church of Jesus Christ will be present on earth during the tribulation or whether God will remove it from the earth just prior to the great tribulation. These two positions, known respectively as posttribulationism and pretribulationism, will receive further attention later.

Christ's second coming will bring Satan and his helpers under control, binding them for one thousand years. Without this, of course, the conditions found in the millennium would be impossible. Near the end of the millennium, however, Satan will be unbound briefly and will launch one desperate, final struggle. Then he

---

2. Ernest F. Kevan, "Millennium," p. 352.
3. Ibid.

and his demons will be utterly vanquished, cast into the lake of fire prepared for them.[4]

The two resurrections of Revelation 20:4–6 are to be distinguished on the basis of their participants, not, as in amillennialism and postmillennialism, on the basis of their natures. Both resurrections, not just the second (as most amillennialists believe), are physical or bodily. Only believers are involved in the first resurrection, however, whereas the rest of the human race, the non-Christians, are not resurrected until the end of the millennium. One reason for dividing the resurrection is that all believers will reign together with Christ during the millennium, those who are alive when Christ returns and those who have died in the faith. The resurrection of unbelievers serves only to get them to the judgment.

While both groups of premillennialists agree on the features enumerated above, they disagree on a number of points. The most significant point is the relationship of the church to the tribulation. The pretribulationist believes that the church will be "raptured," or removed from the world, prior to the great tribulation.[5] The posttribulationist believes that the church will remain in the world during the tribulation, although it may be shielded from some of the tribulation's more severe aspects.[6] A closely related point is the nature of the second coming. Posttribulationism sees it as a single, unitary coming at the end of the tribulation. Pretribulationism sees it as consisting of two states or phases—a "coming for" the church at the beginning of the tribulation, removing it from the world, and a "coming with" the saints at the end of the tribulation.

Other differences are more subtle. One is a matter of attitude. The pretribulationist generally is more interested in the second coming and its timing than is the posttribulationist. In this respect the posttribulationist more closely resembles the amillennialist than he does the pretribulational premillennialist. There also is something of a difference of ethos between the two. Pre-

---

4. Charles L. Feinberg, *Premillennialism or Amillennialism? The Premillennial and Amillennial Systems of Interpretation Analyzed and Compared,* pp. 134–35.

5. Walvoord, *The Rapture Question,* pp. 69–73.

6. Ladd, *The Blessed Hope,* pp. 89ff.

tribulationists, who generally are dispensationalists, frequently have a more Jewish tone to their millennium, their eschatology, and their entire theology than do the posttribulationists.

History of Premillennialism

The view that we today term *premillennialism* has a long history, having roots in the early church. Probably it was the dominant belief during the apostolic period, when Christians believed strongly in the approaching end of the world and the parousia of Jesus Christ. They expected a cataclysmic transformation, not a gradual, progressive coming of the kingdom. This hope was exceedingly intense at times.[7] In the postapostolic period the eschatological hope was still strong, but the Lord's return was thought to be somewhat more distant. There had been something of a disappointment when the expected early return did not materialize, but this had not particularly deterred the faith of these Christians.

Justin Martyr (100?–165?), the apologist, is an example of this period.[8] He regarded belief in the resurrection as indispensable to Christian faith. Those who do not hold this view are not entitled to be called Christians. He noted two subclasses of Christians: those who expect an earthly reign of Christ, centering in a new Jerusalem that is located on the topographical site of the old; and those who expect no millennium. He considered the former to be orthodox and the latter to be flawed in their faith. Justin applied all Old Testament prophecies about the future glory of the chosen people to the intermediary reign of Christ, not to the final consummation, and he interpreted these prophecies in a literalistic fashion. This view, known as chiliasm, is prominent in Justin's theological writings, but it is not mentioned in his apologetic writings. The reason may well have been that belief in a blessed life after death would not complicate Christianity's relationship to the state, while the idea of an earthly theocracy, even though it is to be established without any force, would be much more threatening to civil

---

7. A. J. Visser, "A Bird's-Eye View of Ancient Christian Eschatology," pp. 6–7.

8. Ibid., pp. 8–9.

authority. For the same reason the silence of other apologists—such as Theophilus, Athenagoras, and Tatianus—on the millennial question should not be considered significant.

Irenaeus (130?–200?) also was a definite premillennialist. He was more outspoken than Justin in his criticism and refutation of those who did not accept this position.[9] He also had a more definite rationale for the millennium. The first is that the perfection of believers takes place in connection with the vision of God. The millennial reign of Christ, which occurs between man's condition here and now and the supreme eternal bliss, trains man for this vision. The second is that the victory of Christ would be incomplete if it were only within the world to come. It is necessary that this world also realize God's intentions. The Lord's victory must be celebrated in time before He rules in eternity.

Much of the millennialism of this early period of the church had a rather sensuous flavor. The glories of the millennium would be amplified versions of the blessings of the present life. These conceptions were largely drawn from Jewish eschatological ideas. The earth would be renewed and Jerusalem rebuilt and glorified. Men would be perfectly righteous and happy. There would be no sorrow and no labor. The moon would have the brilliance our sun now has, and the sun would be seven times its present brilliance. The earth would produce abundantly, and a table would always be spread with food.[10]

Some believed that time is to be of six thousand years duration, corresponding to the six days of creation. These men (Irenaeus, Hippolytus, Lactantius, and others, following the Epistle of Barnabas) believed that Christ's first coming had taken place within the sixth thousand-year period and that His second coming would take place at its close. The seventh thousand-year period, the millennium, would then correspond to the day of rest. This meant that the second coming could not be more than one thousand years away. This led to attempts to calculate the date of the second coming. Some concluded from the Book of Daniel that the year A.D. 204 would bring the world to an end. Lactantius thought it

9. Ibid., pp. 9–11.

10. Ibid., pp. 10–11; W. Adams Brown, "Millennium," p. 372; J. A. Mac-Culloch, "Eschatology," pp. 387–88.

would be 200. Another idea, based on the expected duration of the Roman Empire, was that the end would come in 195. Hippolytus based his calculations upon the proportions of the holy ark and determined that it would come in about 500. The Montanists also were millennialists, but they expected the second coming, and with it the millennium, at any moment.[11]

Opposition to this chiliasm arose rather early, particularly in the East. The excesses of Montanism helped to discredit it and to stamp it as Jewish in origin and character rather than Christian. This rejection was due, at least in part, to the chiliasts' ideas of the millennium being so realistic (materialistic) and crass. This certainly helped to repulse the more intellectually inclined Christians like the Alexandrian school—Clement, Origen, and Dionysius—which led the opposition to chiliasm. Origen, who had a tendency to spiritualize conceptions, opposed the chiliasts vigorously. At times the controversy was severe; the Egyptian church nearly split over this issue. What finally prevailed in the East was a moderately spiritualistic view, not as extreme as Origen's but allowing no room for chiliasm.[12]

In the West, chiliasm was quite strong for a considerable period. While never universally accepted, it was a potent force up to Augustine and later. It never completely disappeared. Lactantius (250?–320?), a sophisticated and educated believer, was a chiliast, but he rejected some of the grosser aspects of chiliasm, such as the idea of Nero returning from the dead to be the Antichrist. The reinterpretation of Revelation by Augustine, referred to earlier, proved to be the major factor in the decline of chiliasm in the West. Augustine himself had been a millenarian in his earlier days before coming to his new view. Although Augustine saw the millennium as fulfilled within the church age, he was very tolerant of differing views that were not too gross and carnal. The millennium was not a central and indispensable point of doctrine.[13]

During the Middle Ages some mystical sects revived and kept premillennialism alive. For the most part, however, the Augustinian

11. MacCulloch, "Eschatology," p. 388.

12. Visser, "Ancient Christian Eschatology," pp. 15–19.

13. Ibid., pp. 19–21.

view prevailed. At times premillennialism was tolerated, at other times it was regarded as heretical. In either case, it was very rare.[14]

During the Reformation both Lutheran and Reformed groups for the most part followed Augustine. The radical segment of the Reformation, the Anabaptists, perpetuated the expectation of Christ's earthly reign, however. But, because of some other rather extreme beliefs, the premillennialism of the Anabaptists tended to be disregarded by mainstream Christianity.[15]

It is within conservative circles, and particularly its non-Reformed segments, that premillennialism has experienced great growth during approximately the last one hundred years. Liberals were almost universally postmillennialists (although the converse was by no means true), and many conservatives considered suspect anything associated with liberalism. About this time the dispensational variety of premillennialism arose and, spread especially by the Scofield Reference Bible and Bible institutes, grew rapidly in popularity. Premillennialism, especially this form of it, is very popular today in the more conservative Baptist movements and is almost universally accepted among independent, fundamental churches.

Tenets of Premillennialism

The Two Resurrections

The premillennialist insists that the two resurrections mentioned in Revelation 20:4–6 are both bodily in nature. Because this point forms the linchpin of the premillennial position, it deserves close scrutiny.

A word of explanation regarding hermeneutics is in order as background for understanding this specific passage, and indeed the entire Book of Revelation. The premillennialist adopts a relatively literalistic hermeneutic in interpreting Scripture, and particularly the Apocalypse. This means that the words are taken literally whenever this does not lead to absurdity. Further, premillennialists exhibit a strong tendency toward the futurist interpretation of

---

14. Brown, "Millennium," pp. 372–73.
15. Clarence Beckwith, "Millennium," p. 376.

Revelation, rather than the preterist, historical, or idealist interpretations. The preterist interpretation regards the events of the book as having occurred when the book was written, the historical interpretation regards these events as having been future when the book was written but occurring throughout the history of the church; the idealist or symbolic interpretation dehistoricizes these events, making them purely symbolic of truths that are timeless in character; the futurist interpretation regards these events as primarily occurring in the end time. Dispensational premillennialism follows the futurist method of interpretation almost exclusively. Historical premillennialism, however, represented by such writers as George E. Ladd and G. R. Beasley-Murray, combines the futurist and preterist views, holding that the book necessarily had a message for John's own age and that it represents the consummation of redemptive history. Advocates of both positions believe that, at least in part, to comprehend the message of Revelation is to understand events yet to come.

In his book *Crucial Questions About the Kingdom of God,* as well as in several articles, Ladd has given perhaps the most thorough and emphatic defense of the view that there are two bodily resurrections. He employed several lines of argument, the first and foremost being exegetical. He regards the interpretation of Revelation 20 as reducible to or dependent upon one single question: Are the resurrections in verse 4 and verse 5 both bodily resurrections? Is the first resurrection literal, a resurrection of the body, or spiritual, a resurrection of the soul? The answer rests upon the proper rendering of the term ἔζησαν in verse 4.

The first resurrection involves two groups: the apostles and saints to whom judgment or ruling power has been promised (see Matt. 19:28 and I Cor. 6:3), and the martyrs. There are several reasons why this first resurrection cannot be anything but a literal, bodily resurrection.

1. The interpretation which makes these words refer to the fate of the martyrs after death is quite superfluous. No Christian needed assurance that martyrdom destroys only the body and not the soul. Jesus had made very clear in Matthew 10:28 that only God can harm the soul.[16]

---

16. Ladd, "Revelation 20," p. 169.

2. It is true that the terms *death* and *life* are used of both spiritual and physical existence. Thus it is possible *in principle* that this resurrection is spiritual. When they are used of spiritual death and life, however, there is always some clue in the context to suggest this. Nothing in the context suggests this interpretation. [17]

Because both the first and second resurrections are described in identical terminology, ἔζησαν, [18] and because no qualifying adjectives or adverbs or anything else indicate that the two resurrections are different in kind, the attempt to make them different appears to be purely arbitrary. As Henry Alford put it:

> If, in a passage where *two resurrections* are mentioned, where certain *souls lived* at the first, and the rest of the *dead lived* only at the end of a specified period after that first,—if in such a passage the first resurrection may be understood to mean *spiritual* rising with Christ, while the second means *literal* rising from the grave;—then there is an end of all significance in language, and Scripture is wiped out as a definite testimony to anything. [19]

Beasley-Murray no less vigorously argued that to interpret "they came to life again" (v. 4) as an entirely different kind of resurrection is to attribute confusion and "chaotic thinking" to the author, who supposedly had in mind two different types of resurrection but who gave no indication of a shift of reference. [20]

The description of the two resurrections, Ladd noted, is completely parallel. The verb ἔζησαν elsewhere means "bodily resurrection" (Rev. 2:8; 13:14; Ezek. 37:10). If it means bodily resurrection in verse 5, it must mean the same in verse 4b or "we have lost control of exegesis." [21]

Since the context gives no basis for distinguishing these two, we must not do so unless we can find teachings in the rest of Scripture that demand such a distinction. There are no such teachings, however. The absence of reference either way is essentially a negative

---

17. *Crucial Questions About the Kingdom of God,* p. 146.

18. Ibid., pp. 143–44.

19. *The New Testament for English Readers,* 2 vols. (1863–1866; reprint ed., 2 vols. in 1, Chicago: Moody, n.d.), pp. 1928–29.

20. "The Revelation," p. 1306.

21. "Revelation 20," p. 169.

argument. If there is no additional Scriptural evidence on this matter, then we must interpret the two occurrences of ἔζησαν similarly.[22]

Further, we should note that those who participate in the second resurrection apparently were not involved in the first. These are "the rest" (οἱ λοιποί), those who remain or who did not participate in the first resurrection. While there is some ambiguity about this expression, it does not appear to exclude the latter group from the former.[23]

In addition to this passage, there are, Ladd claimed, other passages that seem to hint at the possibility of more than one resurrection. Philippians 3:11 speaks of ἐξανάστασιν τὴν ἐκ νεκρῶν, literally the "out-resurrection out from among dead ones," a meaning that is generally lost in English translations, which say something like, "a resurrection from (or of) the dead." Paul seems in this text to have been aspiring to a resurrection that will, in effect, result in a separation from dead persons. Luke 14:14 refers to a resurrection of the righteous, evidently implying a distinction from resurrection in general. Luke 20:35 speaks of resurrection from the dead, similar in import to Philippians 3:11, except that this is not an "out-resurrection." Ladd said that I Corinthians 15:23 and I Thessalonians 4:16 also hint at a partial resurrection, and Daniel 12:2 and John 5:29 suggest a resurrection in two stages.[24]

Ladd also argued for the millennium on theological grounds. Although some critics of premillennialism have objected that a millennium is superfluous, Ladd contended that it plays a definite and integral part in the plan of God. It is a further stage in God's redemptive purpose in Christ. During His life on earth, Christ experienced the state of humiliation in progressive stages. Following His resurrection and ascension, He reassumed the glory and power which had been His, reigning at the Father's right hand. His reign of triumph is not yet apparent, however. If it is to be fully exercised and demonstrated, it must become public in power and glory. Ladd believes that it is necessary for this manifestation of Christ's

22. Ladd, *The Kingdom of God,* pp. 169ff.

23. Ibid., pp. 148–49.

24. Ibid., p. 183. Cf. Feinberg, *Premillennialism or Amillennialism?,* pp. 229–35.

glory and sovereignty to take place upon the earth. This is the purpose served by the millennium. Ladd discerned three stages in Christ's triumph over death as described in I Corinthians 15:23–26: the resurrection, the second coming (the parousia), and the end (the telos).[25] The interval between the resurrection and the parousia is the church age; the interval between the parousia and the telos—without which the two might as well be collapsed into one—is the millennium. The former is the age of the Son's hidden rule; the latter, the age of His manifested rule.[26]

For the dispensational premillennialist there is yet another argument for the millennium: the large number of prophecies, particularly in the Old Testament, still unfulfilled. The dispensationalist believes that no Old Testament prophecies are fulfilled within the church age and that some of these prophecies are of such a nature that they must occur upon earth. There must therefore be some period or interlude upon the earth when these prophecies can be fulfilled, namely, an earthly millennium. From these prophecies many details of the millennial rule of Christ are drawn.[27]

The Nature of the Millennium

Although there are variations, there are in all premillennial views of the millennium certain common elements. The first is obviously that during this period Jesus Christ will possess absolute control. The major forces opposing Him and His rule during the period between His ascension and His second coming will have been, for all practical purposes, eliminated. Satan will have been restrained. Antichrist (the beast) and the false prophet will have been destroyed by Christ at His second coming. As a result, all who are alive during this period will submit to the rule of the Messiah. Every knee will bow, as Paul expressed it in Philippians 2:10–11.[28]

This will be a period of righteous rule. The standard of life envisioned in the Sermon on the Mount will become a reality. The

---

25. "Revelation 20," p. 171.

26. "The Revelation of Christ's Glory," p. 14.

27. Walvoord, "Dispensational Premillennialism," p. 13.

28. Feinberg, *Premillennialism or Amillennialism?*, pp. 142–43; Ladd, "The Revelation of Christ's Glory," p. 168.

concern will not be merely with what a person does—his outward actions—but with what he is—his thoughts and intentions. Christ will reign with justice over His subjects.[29]

This reign of Christ will involve a political dimension, a world-wide peace. This in itself will mark the millennium as clearly distinct from the rest of history. Within the span of recorded history, worldwide peace has, on the average, prevailed about one year in fifteen. Some wars have been great global conflicts; some have been much more limited in scope. Seldom, however, has there been genuine universal peace. When the Prince of Peace comes, however, peace will prevail. In prophetic language, swords shall be beaten into plowshares and spears into pruning hooks, and nation will not raise sword against nation (Isa. 2:4; Mic. 4:3). This will not be *detente,* or mere absence of outward hostilities, but genuine harmony.[30]

There will also be harmony within the creation. The curse that was pronounced upon man because of the fall also affected the rest of the creation. Nature is pictured as "groaning and travailing," waiting for its redemption and release (Rom. 8:22—23). This will be accomplished by the return of Christ. In the millennium hostility among creatures will cease (Isa. 11:8—9; 65:25). Man will not need to fear any creature. The destructive forces of nature such as storms, earthquakes, and volcanoes will be stilled. The picture of Jesus calming the sea by rebuking the storm (Matt. 8:26) is an anticipation of what will most fully occur at the time of the millennium.[31]

Further, the saints will reign together with Christ. In Revelation 20 those who are raised in the first resurrection reign with Christ during the millennium. The exact nature of their rule is not spelled out (i.e., the subjects, the degree of control, and the aspects of life and behavior involved). It does appear, however, that a reward for their faithfulness will be to share or participate in what Jesus Christ does.

---

29. Ladd, *The Kingdom of God,* p. 126.

30. Feinberg, *Premillennialism or Amillennialism?,* pp. 145–46.

31. Ibid., p. 147; Loraine Boettner, *The Millennium,* pp. 290–91.

Israel in the Millennium

Finally, premillennialists see a special status for Israel during the millennium, though they disagree concerning the exact nature of this status.

On the one hand, dispensational premillennialists hold that there will be a virtual restoration of the Old Testament economy. According to this view God has only temporarily turned from His prime dealings with national Israel to the church, or spiritual Israel. God turned away because Israel rejected Christ's offer of the kingdom. When God has accomplished His purpose in connection with the church, however, He will resume His relations with Israel. In the millennium Israel will be restored to the land of Palestine. Jesus will sit upon the literal throne of David and rule the world from Jerusalem. The Old Testament temple worship and priestly order will be restored, including the sacrificial system. Into the millennium is placed the fulfillment of virtually all Old Testament prophecies not fulfilled by the time of Christ, or at least by Pentecost.[32]

On the other hand, a historical premillennialist like Ladd places considerably less emphasis upon national Israel than do the dispensationalists. He believes that the church has become the spiritual Israel and that many of the prophecies and promises relating to Israel are now fulfilled in the church. The Old Testament sacrificial system has forever passed away because Christ, the reality, has come. Nonetheless, he believes that literal or national Israel is yet to be saved. He bases this primarily upon Romans 11:15–16. In the future Israel will turn to Christ and be saved. Not every single Israelite will be converted, but the nation as a whole will be. Through the agency of Israel, God will bless the whole world, and presumably this will occur during the millennium.[33]

Evaluation of Premillennialism

In our evaluation of premillennialism, we will by-pass the criticisms that apply only to one or another variety of pre-

---

32. Feinberg, *Premillennialism or Amillennialism?*, p. 146; Walvoord, *The Millennial Kingdom*, p. 302.

33. "Israel and the Church," pp. 206–13.

millennialism and confine ourselves to those features common to premillennialism in general.

Positive Aspects

On the positive side, premillennialists have displayed more eschatological earnestness than have many representatives of competitive systems. To be sure, premillennialists have sometimes carried this to extreme lengths, showing an excessive interest in future things and indulging in undue speculation about details that we can never resolve with the data currently available. Nonetheless the Bible does place great emphasis on the age to come, and premillennialists certainly have not neglected this emphasis.

Further, premillennialists have taken exegesis seriously. Perhaps the most minute scrutiny of the relevant Biblical texts, and particularly of the Book of Revelation, has been done by premillennialists. This might be attributable to their more literal approach to interpreting prophetic writings, an approach that tends to make one more optimistic regarding the possibility of determining the meaning of these writings. If we believe the Scriptures to be authoritative, we must consider this intensive exegesis (whatever the reason for it) a very positive value.

Finally, it appears that the premillennial interpretation of the crucial verses in Revelation 20 is more adequate and raises fewer difficulties than do alternative interpretations.

Negative Aspects

On the other hand, certain problems do attach to the premillennial scheme, and these need to be carefully examined as well.

One objection is the sparseness of Biblical references to the millennium. It is explicitly referred to only in Revelation 20. Surely if this is as important a doctrine as premillennialists claim, it ought to be mentioned more than once in the whole of Scripture. Premillennialists reply that numerous other passages, many of them prophecies, refer to the millennium. Yet these alone are not sufficiently clear and unambiguous to lead us to believe in a millennium.

Jesus had much to say about the last things: many of His parables related to this subject, and one whole discourse, Matthew

24–25, was devoted to the end times. Yet He certainly never predicted a thousand-year earthly reign, nor did He predict any events that require such a period to be fulfilled. Similarly, when Paul treated the second coming, he made no mention of an earthly rule. Some therefore find it better to understand the lone millennial reference in some way other than as a literal, earthly, thousand-year period.

Another objection is the relatively literal way premillennialists interpret Old Testament prophecies. Dispensationalists, of course, apply this hermeneutic more stringently and thoroughly than do historical premillennialists. Hence dispensationalists insist that prophecies regarding Israel must be fulfilled by literal, national Israel, while historical premillennialists see at least some of these prophecies being fulfilled by the church, or spiritual Israel. The premillennialist tends to argue that since the prophecies already fulfilled were fulfilled in rather literal fashion, prophecies not yet fulfilled will be fulfilled in the same manner. He decries attempts to allegorize prophecy.

Some fulfilled prophecies, however, have not been fulfilled very literally, as Louis Berkhof pointed out.[34] The prediction that Elijah would precede the coming of the Messiah was fulfilled by John the Baptist, not the actual, literal, Old Testament character. Peter argued that the promise to David that the resurrected Christ would sit upon his throne was fulfilled when Jesus was raised from the dead and exalted at the right hand of God (Acts 2:29–36). The praying church saw in the imprisonment of Peter and John a fulfillment of Psalm 2, which depicts kings and rulers as opposing the King whom God had set upon His holy hill of Zion (Acts 4:21–28). At the great council of Jerusalem, James declared that Amos, in speaking of the restoration of the fallen tabernacle of David, had referred to the spiritual establishment of the kingdom and the ingathering of the Gentiles (Acts 15:13–18). Other passages that seem to handle prophetic fulfillment similarly include Matthew 2:16–18, Acts 2:14–21, and Galatians 4:27. Premillennialists sometimes say that prophecies like these may have both literal and spiritual fulfillment. Thus, for example, Acts 15 is

---

34. *The Kingdom of God: The Development of the Idea of the Kingdom, Especially Since the Eighteenth Century,* p. 165.

saying that God will first gather the Gentiles and then later re-establish the Davidic kingdom. Such interpretations, however, indicate a weakness in the premillennial approach to prophetic Scriptures.

A further problem is that an earthly millennium is theologically superfluous, a point raised especially by amillennialists. Why should there be an earthly reign of Christ at all? Why should we not move directly from the second coming of Christ to the judgment and then to the ultimate states of destiny of both the righteous and the unrighteous? Even Ladd's argument that there must be an earthly reign to demonstrate the supremacy of Christ is unpersuasive, for could not Christ's supremacy also be demonstrated by the establishment of an eternal spiritual kingdom? Particularly in view of the sparcity of textual references, the millennium seems dispensable.

Further, the way in which the kingdom will be established seems to conflict in some ways with other Biblical conceptions. According to premillennial teaching, the kingdom will be inaugurated by a dramatic, forceful demonstration of the power of the Lord, executing judgment upon the world and establishing His reign by the iron rod. This, however, seems to contradict the way in which God works now, through the quiet, internal, invisible operation of the Holy Spirit, changing the hearts of men from within. Jesus, indeed, said that His kingdom is not of this world, and that if it were, His servants would fight (John 18:36). Yet premillennialism sees Christ as ruling with a rod of iron. Not merely the timing, but the very means of the establishment of the kingdom in the premillennial view appears to differ from the conception Jesus gives in John 18.

Finally, premillennialism's (especially dispensationalism's) tendency to give the millennium a Jewish flavor has been criticized for centuries, two early critics being Caius of Rome (ca. 200) and Origen. The premillennialist must be on guard lest literal Israel retain such a significant place in God's plan and program that it virtually displaces the church as the primary object of God's working. He must also beware of interpreting the New Testament with the Old, thereby nullifying progressive revelation.

Part 3

Tribulational Views

Chapter 6

Dispensationalism

Before examining the various tribulational views, we need to notice the theological and hermeneutical system known as dispensationalism. Some regard it as tantamount to pretribulationism, but this identification needs to be qualified in two respects: First, dispensationalism is more than a view of the relationship of Christ's coming to the tribulation. It is a whole system of theology, of which eschatology is but one part. Further, it is a method of interpreting the Bible, therefore affecting one's understanding of even nondoctrinal portions of the Scripture. And second, while all dispensationalists are pretribulationists, not all pretribulationists are dispensationalists.

Nonetheless, it is important to examine this entire system and scheme before proceeding to the tribulational views. Dispensationalism is a widely influential position within American fundamentalism, and once one accepts dispensationalism the question of the tribulation is effectively closed.

Because the rise of dispensationalism roughly paralleled that of the fundamentalist movement, it became virtually the official theology of fundamentalism. Some commentators have practically identified the two. Some proponents of dispensationalism consider it to be not an interpretation of the Bible, but simply a restatement of what the Bible says. Some have made it a test of orthodoxy, regarding one who fails to hold all of its points as one who denies Scripture itself. In many cases a whole mind set or collection of attitudes is involved.

109

In this connection we need to note that the various elements are essential parts of an organic whole. Some consider the question of a pre- or posttribulational rapture a relatively independent issue. For the dispensationalist, however, the truth of the dispensational system implies the truth of pretribulationism, and the falsity of pretribulationalism implies the falsity of dispensationalism. For such a person, then, an attack upon pretribulationism appears to be an attack upon the whole Christian system of belief. His entire Christian experience has been associated with this way of believing, and even conditioned to particular terms and expressions. While this is true of adherents of all systems of belief and life, it is particularly the case with dispensationalists, among whom there generally is quite extensive and specific doctrinal instruction, approaching (in some cases) indoctrination. We must therefore bear in mind that their sense of religious security is bound up with what appear to them to be essentials of Christianity.

Overview of Dispensationalism

We should look at the overall pattern of dispensationalism and define it before scrutinizing it more closely. To some extent we will seek also to remove some misconceptions and even caricatures of dispensationalism that have sometimes been held.

First is the belief that there are different *dispensations,* a word defined by Charles C. Ryrie as "a distinguishable economy in the outworking of God's purpose."[1] It is a stewardship of God's light, a step in the revelation of God's truth. Who can deny that at the call of Abraham or the call of Moses (the burning-bush incident) there was a genuinely new outpouring of revelation? The same is true of the coming of Christ and of Pentecost. These events shed new light, and the relationship between God and His people changed accordingly.

Also important is the dispensational conception of salvation.[2] Salvation is by faith. It has always been that way, and it always will be, for there is no other way of salvation. Some critics of dispensationalism have imputed to its supporters a belief in new ways or channels of salvation. More correctly, however, dispensationalists

---

1. *Dispensationalism Today,* p. 29.   2. Ibid., pp. 123ff.

say that while new light has been shed upon the relationship between God and man, no new way of entering into that relationship has ever been instituted. To be sure, some ultra-dispensationalists may have believed and taught otherwise, but mainline dispensationalists insist upon this unity of salvation—the new birth is common to all periods of God's dealing with mankind. No one ever enters into God's fellowship without faith and the new birth.

Further, the moral law of God, unlike the ceremonial law, applies to all dispensations,[3] though of course it may be differently applied at different times. The prohibition of killing, for example, is not restricted to any one dispensation; murder of other humans has always been and always will be wrong. Sometimes dispensationalists insist that a passage must be applied only to the dispensation to which it is addressed. Hence, teachings about life under the ceremonial law or life in the millennium are not to be applied now. The moral law is always in effect, however, although its exact content may vary. To sum up: the saints in various ages have more points in common than points of difference.

History of Dispensationalism

The dispensationalist movement is of fairly recent origin. No trace of this theology can be found in the early history of the church. For several reasons, however, this in itself should not bear too strongly upon the question of the truth of dispensationalism.

First, many doctrines were not articulated by the church for many centuries. This is true of the person and work of Christ, the Trinity, and virtually all other doctrines as well. For the most part, beliefs were held implicitly and only became explicit when a deviant form of teaching arose or when a controversy broke out in the church. Eschatology in particular has not been elaborated in detail until rather recently.

Further, other methods of Bible study and interpretation, including some employed by opponents of dispensationalism, are also of relatively recent origin. One example is literary and historical criticism of the Bible.

---

3. Ibid., p. 108.

Third, if we are making any progress in the study of the Bible, we must expect some things to be uncovered that were not previously known. This may involve interpretations of specific passages, but it may well also lead to a whole new system of theology. To deny this undercuts all possibility of real progress in Biblical and theological understanding.

To reject dispensationalism because of its apparent novelty is, therefore, a weak argument. We can, nevertheless, examine the movement's history in order to respond to those who argue for its truth on the basis of its antiquity.

The advocates of dispensationalism generally acknowledge that it was not a full-blown system until the twentieth century, but they argue that there were significant forerunners of this system. To be sure, the premillennialism of the church's first centuries may have included belief in a pretribulational rapture of the church. Moreover, some of these early premillennialists spoke of dispensations. They did not mean by *dispensation,* however, quite what dispensationalists today mean by it. Even John Calvin referred to dispensations, but he was no dispensationalist.

Some writers have certainly divided Biblical history into periods or eras. Some of these schemes were quite simple and contained relatively few such periods. William Cave (1633–1713), for example, spoke of the patriarchal, mosaical, and evangelical periods.[4] Pierre Poiret (1646–1719), however, listed six periods or "oeconomies"—creation, sin, restoration before the incarnation of Christ, restoration after the incarnation, cooperation with the operation of God, and universal providence.[5] While these divisions served to distinguish periods of time, they did not distinguish ways of God's working.

The real developer of dispensational hermeneutics and theology was John Nelson Darby (1800–1882).[6] Darby was born of Irish parents in London in November 1800. His early years were spent

---

4. *The Lives of the Apostles, and the Two Evangelists Saint Mark and Saint Luke.*

5. *The Divine Oeconomy; or, An Universal System of the Works and Purposes of God Towards Men, Demonstrated.*

6. For this entire section on Darby, see Clarence B. Bass, *Backgrounds to Dispensationalism: Its Historical Genesis and Ecclesiastical Implications,* pp. 49–51.

and his basic education obtained in Ireland. Darby trained for the law and began to practice it in 1822, apparently capable of excelling in this profession. Shortly thereafter, however, he was converted, and he left the profession after only one year of practice. His interest in theology and the church grew, and in 1825 he was ordained a deacon of the Church of England. He worked very hard as the curate of a parish in Ennisbury, and his labors were rewarded by many conversions of Roman Catholics.

While in Dublin to be ordained to the ministry, he learned that the bishop there had issued and the clergy endorsed a decree denouncing Roman Catholics and claiming special favors and protection for the Church of England. This decree also required a pledge of allegiance to the king, on the contention that Catholics owe their first loyalty to the king, not the pope. This greatly disturbed Darby and put him in a dilemma: on the one hand, he would not disobey the diocesan rule; on the other hand, allegiance to the king seemed little better than devotion to the pope. In the midst of this attempt to establish the Church of England, he became involved with what was known as the Brethren movement.

Two basic principles distinguished this movement: first, every Lord's Day is set aside for "breaking of bread"; second, one serves in the ministry by the call of Christ, not by the ordination of man. It is significant that Darby was exposed to this latter concept when he was preparing for ordination in the Church of England and when he was having questions of conscience about obeying the decree of the bishop. He continued to minister in the Church of England for a time, but he eventually left that church.

Darby rather quickly became active in the Brethren movement. Although he had not founded it, his great organizational abilities soon made him its leader and organizer, forming groups in various places. The group at Plymouth was the first to bear the name *brethren,* and they came to be known as "the brethren at Plymouth," or simply, "Plymouth Brethren." That term came to be applied to the other groups as well. Through something of an accident of history, these people who merely wanted to be known as "brothers in Christ" came to be known as Plymouth Brethren, a title with something of a denominational overtone.

Darby, a prolific writer, developed Brethren thought into a system. Others followed in the Darby line of interpretation: for

113

example, C. H. Mackintosh, whose books often listed only the initials C. H. M. on the title page; G. Campbell Morgan, although he later abandoned the dispensational approach; Harry Ironside; A. C. Gaebelein; and C. I. Scofield. All of these men effectively popularized the dispensational approach, their extensive writings being widely read in fundamentalist circles.

Probably the most effective popularization of dispensationalism was the Scofield Reference Bible. Early in the twentieth century there were few Bibles available with "helps." Try to imagine the predicament of the typical layman. He knows some Bible stories but is doubtful about their chronological order or geographical setting, or, even more likely, he is doubtful about the meaning of many doctrinal passages. So when he obtains a Bible with an outline right with the text and explanatory notes at the foot of the page, he is delighted. This naturally has a strong appeal to anyone who lacks a commentary or who finds it inconvenient to carry a commentary with him. Scofield (1843–1921) had conveniently combined text and commentary into one volume. It is not surprising that some persons found it difficult to remember whether they had read something at the bottom of the page (in the notes) or in the middle (in the text). Scofield's interpretation became widely adopted in fundamentalist circles. In some churches one can even hear the rustling of many pages being turned simultaneously because so many persons carry the Scofield Bible. It is not unheard of for a pastor to give the location of a passage, not by book, chapter, and verse, but by page number!

The other effective means of this system's propagation was Bible institutes. Many fundamentalist congregations had at one time been part of large denominations and had drawn their ministers, either directly or indirectly, from the seminaries of those denominations. When indications of doctrinal deviation appeared in these seminaries, however, churches began to draw their ministers not from the seminaries but from Bible institutes. Almost without exception these institutions and their faculties were steeped in dispensationalism. Thus, this view spread even more widely. In some cases the Bible institutes evolved into Bible colleges and then into Christian liberal arts colleges: for example, Providence Bible Institute became Providence-Barrington Bible College and then Barrington College. Some also developed a theological seminary: the Bible Institute of Los Angeles became Biola College but also spawned Talbot Theological Seminary. Dallas Theological Seminary had a somewhat different but nonetheless basically similar pattern of development. Hence ministerial students did not have to choose between a seminary education and a thoroughly evangelical theological education. Some students obtained their undergraduate education at a Bible college and then went to a dispensational seminary, such as Dallas, Talbot, Grace, or Western Conservative Baptist.

Tenets of Dispensationalism

The Interpretation of Scripture

The first tenet of dispensationalism is that the Bible must be interpreted literally.[7] To appreciate this fully, one must recognize that dispensationalism arose when higher criticism was developing. This latter method of getting at the Bible's meaning in some cases rested upon rationalistic presuppositions. One rationalistic presupposition was that no supernatural event can occur. As an example, Jesus' supposed walking on water (Matt. 14:22–33) occurred on a foggy day. Jesus was actually standing on the shore, but in the fog one could not discern the beach. Hence Jesus appeared to be standing on the water itself. Such an approach gives a meaning to the Bible quite in contrast with its more obvious or apparent meaning. For many, then, "nonliteral" came to be identified with "liberal."

In this context it is understandable that dispensationalists attempted to take the Scripture as literally as possible. To be sure, they did not understand literally certain obviously figurative expressions, such as trees clapping their hands (Isa. 55:12). Nonetheless, the Scripture is to be taken literally whenever this does not result in a ludicrous situation. A slogan most dispensationalists would gladly adopt and endorse is: When the plain sense makes good sense, seek no other sense.

This is particularly the case when interpreting Biblical references to Israel. The term *Israel* must always refer to the actual nation

---

7. Ryrie, *Dispensationalism Today*, pp. 86–89; John F. Walvoord, "Dispensational Premillennialism," pp. 11–12.

Israel, ethnic Israel, the Israel that traces its physical descent back to Jacob (or, as God came to call him, Israel). It never refers to "spiritual Israel."[8]

All prophetic Scripture is to be treated similarly. All prophecy will be fulfilled literally and in detail. If the Bible says that Christ, having descended, will stand upon the Mount of Olives and that the mountain will split, then Christ will literally stand upon the literal mountain and the mountain will literally split.

Concomitant with this literal interpretation of prophecy is a typological interpretation of historical or narrative passages, which at times strongly resembles the old allegorical method. Types are found in such profusion and given such esoteric meanings that the dispensationalist goes far beyond the literal meaning of the events recited. One example is the interpretation of the Book of Esther propounded by Walter Scott, whom Scofield called "the eminent Bible teacher":

> As to the typical bearing of the book, Ahasuerus would represent the supreme Gentile authority, and Vashti, "beauty," the professing Church, failing to show her beauty. She is then superceded by the Jewish bride, Esther, "star," while the wicked Hamann, planning the destruction of Israel, in the midst of his murderous purposes, signally cut off, would as surely figure the conspiracy of the latter day enemies of restored Israel. Mordecai would set forth our Lord, head of his exalted people in the millennial future.[9]

That is supposedly what the historical narrative teaches. The typology found there goes far beyond the literal meaning of the passage. Similarly, the Song of Solomon is often understood as a picture of the relationship of Christ to the church. The description of the tabernacle is seen as being more than just a prescription of the size, color, and shape of the various elements in that structure. It is understood as presenting spiritual truths. When this author was a young pastor in Chicago, he participated in a union Good Friday service. The speaker chose his text for an expository Good Friday sermon from Exodus 39 and found in the description of the high

---

8. Walvoord, "Israel's Restoration," p. 409.

9. *Bible Outlines: Comprehensive Epitomes of the Leading Features of the Old and New Testaments* (London, 1879), p. 113.

priest's breastplate the entire plan of salvation. Every item of the breastplate possessed a special, symbolic significance that was not at all apparent upon a surface reading of the passage.

This is not to suggest that typology is unique to dispensational hermeneutics. Many other Biblical exegetes have also found types within the Bible.[10] Generally they do so, however, only where the context indicates that a type is involved, particularly when a New Testament writer identifies a type within the Old Testament (as the writer of Hebrews does with Melchizedek). The dispensationalist, however, often goes well beyond this, designating as a type that which is not so identified in its context.

Israel and the Church

A second major tenet of dispensationalism is a sharp and definite distinction between Israel and the church. This is regarded as basic to any correct understanding of Scripture. "Indeed, ecclesiology, or the doctrine of the Church," Ryrie said, "is the touchstone of dispensationalism."[11] In this view God made a special covenant with Israel (originally with Abraham) that is unconditional. If it were conditional, its fulfillment would depend upon the obedience of Israel to God's commands. If Israel were disobedient, the promises would be lost and the special relationship would cease. Being *unconditional,* the promises of God *will* come to pass. Regardless of the response of Israel, they will remain God's special people and ultimately receive His blessing.

Several lines of evidence are adduced in arguing for this distinctiveness of Israel. The first is that national Israel and the Gentiles are contrasted in the New Testament.[12] Israel was addressed as a nation in contrast to the Gentiles *after* the church had been established at Pentecost (Acts 3:12; 4:8, 10; 5:21, 31, 35; 21:28). In Romans 10:1 Paul prayed for Israel, a clear reference to Israel as a natural people distinct from and outside the church.

---

10. E.g., Patrick Fairbairn, *The Typology of Scripture, Viewed in Connection with the Whole Series of the Divine Dispensations.*

11. *Dispensationalism Today,* p. 132.

12. Ibid., pp. 137–38.

Further, natural Israel and the church are also contrasted in the New Testament.[13] Paul wrote: "Give no offense to Jews or to Greeks or to the church of God" (I Cor. 10:32). If at this point the Jewish people were simply the same as the Gentiles or the church, what is the point of such a distinction? In Romans 9:3–4 Paul ascribed the covenants and promises to his "kinsmen according to the flesh," obviously referring to natural Israel. These words were written after the beginning of the church, proof that the church did not simply take over the promises and blessings made to Israel. Also, believing Jews and believing Gentiles, who together make up the church in this age, continue to be distinguished in the New Testament. This proves that the term *Israel* still means the physical descendants of Abraham. Paul said in Romans 9:6, "For not all who are descended from Israel belong to Israel." The term *Israel* does not here refer to the church. It simply distinguishes the nation as a whole from the believing element *within the nation.*[14]

Ryrie is aware of the argument of nondispensationalists based upon Galatians 6:15–16: "For in Christ Jesus neither circumcision availeth any thing, nor uncircumcision, but a new creature. And as many as walk according to this rule, peace be on them, and mercy, and (καὶ) upon the Israel of God" (KJV). The question is, Who is "the Israel of God"? The amillennialist (so Ryrie identified all who differ with him on this point of interpretation) insists that it is the entire church. The premillennialist, on the other hand, asserts that Paul was simply singling out Christian Jews for special recognition, not equating "Israel" with the church. The whole issue, according to Ryrie, turns upon the meaning of the conjunction καὶ ("and").[15] It can be taken in the ascensive sense, "even," which would make the church "the Israel of God." It can be taken in the emphatic sense, "and especially" (cf. Mark 16:7; Acts 1:14), which would make "Israel" (Jewish Christians) a very important part of the whole (the church). And it can be taken as a simple connective, "and," which would also make "Israel" refer to Jewish Christians rather than to the whole church. Ryrie noted that only the first or ascensive interpretation ("even") identifies the church and Israel.

13. Ibid., p. 138.
14. Ibid.
15. Ibid., p. 139.

In Ryrie's judgment the question must be decided not by grammar alone but by the argument of the book as a whole, and this favors the connective or emphatic sense of καί. If the New Testament writers meant to equate Israel and the church, they could easily have done so in numerous other places. Ryrie concluded: "Use of the words *Israel* and *Church* shows clearly that in the New Testament national Israel continues with her own promises and the Church is never equated with a so-called "new Israel" but is carefully and continually distinguished as a separate work of God in this age."[16]

The implication is that the term *Israel* is always to be understood in the most literal fashion possible—namely, as ethnic, national, and political Israel—and never in a spiritualized sense—namely, the church. This means that all of God's promises to Abraham and his seed must be literally fulfilled in the actual people of Israel, the nation. Since some of these promises have not yet been fully accomplished, they will be at some future time. Thus, God must yet have a time of special dealing with His covenant nation, Israel.

The church is, according to dispensationalism, totally unforeseen in the Old Testament. This is partly because it is an entity distinctive to this present age and partly because of its basis or manner of origin. Ryrie advanced three proofs of the church's distinctiveness:[17]

1. The mysteriousness of the church. Paul described a mystery "hidden for ages and generations but now made manifest to his saints" (Col. 1:26). The body of Christ is spoken of in the context three times (vv. 18, 22, 24). If the church was an unknown mystery in Old Testament times, it must not have been constituted in that period. In fact, Paul said clearly that this entity is a "new man" (Eph. 2:15) whose existence was made possible only by the death of Christ.

2. Paul's remarks on the beginning of the church. Paul taught emphatically that there is a necessary relationship between the church and the resurrection and ascension of Christ. The church is built upon His resurrection, for the Lord was made Head of the

---

16. Ibid., p. 140.
17. Ibid., pp. 135–37.

church after God "raised him from the dead and made him sit at his right hand in the heavenly places" (Eph. 1:20; cf. vv. 22–23). Further, proper functioning of the body is dependent upon the giving of gifts to the body, which is in turn dependent upon the ascension of Christ (Eph. 4:7–12). If in some way the body of Christ existed before His ascension, it must have been a non-operating body. Built upon the resurrection and ascension, the church must necessarily be distinctive to this age. By the phrase "dead in Christ" (I Thess. 4:16), Paul clearly distinguished those who have died after Christ's first advent from those who died before it, thus further marking off the church as distinct to this age and hidden to Old Testament believers.

3. The baptizing work of the Holy Spirit. The church did not begin until Pentecost. The Lord at His ascension spoke of the baptism of the Holy Spirit as yet future and unlike anything His disciples had previously experienced (Acts 1:5). Acts 2 does not specify that the baptism of the Spirit occurred on the day of Pentecost, but Acts 11:15–16 does, saying that it fulfilled the promise of the Lord. Paul explained that this baptism places people into the body of Christ (I Cor. 12:13). The first occurrence of this baptism was on the day of Pentecost. Since the church is the body of Christ (Col. 1:18), it could not have begun until Pentecost and it must have begun on that day.

Ryrie was careful to point out that the distinctiveness of the church to this age does not mean: (1) that there were no people rightly related to God in Old Testament times, or (2) that Christ did not found the church. All that dispensationalists affirm is that the people of God who have been baptized into the body of Christ and who thus form the church are distinct from saints of earlier days and saints of a future time.[18]

This means that the church is nowhere mentioned in the Old Testament, nowhere prophesied. It is a "parenthesis," coming, specifically, between the sixty-ninth and seventieth weeks of Daniel. No prophecy has been fulfilled since the time of Christ. The prophetic clock has not ticked since Pentecost.[19]

---

18. Ibid., p. 137.

19. Walvoord, *The Rapture Question,* pp. 23–27; Charles L. Feinberg, *Premillennialism or Amillennialism? The Premillennial and Amillennial Systems of Interpretation Analyzed and Compared,* p. 116.

This involves the postponement of the kingdom. Both John the Baptist and Jesus preached that the kingdom was at hand. This earthly kingdom was offered to the Jews, the chosen covenant people, and they rejected it. Dispensationalists do not identify the exact time and place of rejection. Scofield suggested that the kingdom was morally rejected in Matthew 11:20–21, when Jesus began to preach a new message, one of rest and service, to any in the nation who were conscious of need. Yet the final rejection, said Scofield, was later (Matt. 27:31–37). Some place it in Acts 28.[20]

After Israel rejected the kingdom, God offered it to the church. The church was, as it were, God's substitute for Israel, "grafted in." The kingdom for Israel, however, was merely postponed. It will again be offered to God's people, Israel, after the time of the Gentiles is complete. God has not forgotten His people Israel nor displaced them with the church.[21]

The Two Kingdoms

Dispensationalism distinguishes between the kingdom of God and the kingdom of heaven, basing this distinction largely upon the fact that most of the parables of the kingdom (of heaven) in Matthew 13 are not found in Mark and Luke. The kingdom of heaven, according to Scofield, is Jewish, messianic, and Davidic.[22] It had been promised to David, and this promise entered the New Testament period "absolutely unchanged."[23] It was "at hand" from the beginning of John the Baptist's ministry to "the virtual rejection of the King," and then it was postponed. It will be realized in the millennium.

The kingdom of God, on the other hand, is universal. It includes "all moral intelligences willingly subject to the will of God, whether angels, the Church, or saints of past or future dispensations." All dispensations of human history may properly be

---

20. *The Scofield Reference Bible* (New York: Oxford University, 1909), p. 1011 (n. 1).

21. A. C. Gaebelein, *"Hath God Cast Away His People?,"* p. 158.

22. *The Scofield Reference Bible,* p. 996 (n. 1).

23. Ibid., p. 1226 (n. 3).

called dispensations of the kingdom of God. It is the more inclusive of the two terms.[24]

The Purpose of the Millennium

Finally, in dispensationalism the millennium is more than merely a thousand-year reign of Christ on the earth. It has a clear, definite place in the plan of God: the restoration of national Israel to its favored place in God's program and the fulfillment of God's promises to Israel. The millennium therefore has a very Jewish tone. It is the time when Israel really comes into her own. Whereas in some other forms of premillennialism the purpose of the millennium is rather unclear, in dispensationalism it is an integral part of one's theology and of one's understanding of the Bible. Large portions of prophecy are still unfulfilled, and the millennium provides a time for their fulfillment.

Evaluation of Dispensationalism

Positive Aspects

The first strength and benefit of the dispensational system is that it is indeed a system. The word *system* evokes a negative reaction in many circles today, largely because of the influence of existentialism which is hostile to structure and order in reality and to the intellectualizing or rationalizing of truth. From the time of Sören Kierkegaard's attack upon Georg Hegel's system, in which everything fit neatly in its place, existentialism has been suspicious of any treatment of reality that brings the various elements into a coherent whole. Consequently, Biblical studies in recent years have been rather fragmentary in nature, emphasizing Biblical theology and minimizing systematic theology. The dispensationalists, however, have attempted to synthesize or integrate the entire Biblical witness into a unified whole. They have sought to prevent the confusion that the layman experiences when he is told that one portion of Scripture means one thing, and that another portion means the exact opposite. The fact that meaning is best apprehended and understanding best facilitated within a structure, or

---

24. Ibid., p. 1003 (n. 1).

Gestalt, may account at least in part for the great popularity of dispensationalism among lay people.

Second, dispensationalism has attempted to take seriously the idea of progressive revelation and has developed a theology based upon it. The dispensational structure is sometimes graphically pictured as a stairway, each of the dispensations being another step upward. Surely God has revealed more truth as time has elapsed, and dispensationalism recognizes this fact in a formal fashion.

Third, dispensationalism has attempted to be genuinely and thoroughly Biblical. The dispensationalist asks on any point of doctrine, "What does the Bible say?" When he discusses the issues, he speaks in terms of specific Scriptures and demonstrates a thorough knowledge of Bible content. Dispensational schools stress the importance of knowing what the Bible says and where it says it. If the Bible is the supreme authority in matters of faith and practice, then this thorough biblicism must be regarded as a definite virtue.

Negative Aspects

Dispensationalism also has its problems. The first is that despite its attempt to take progressive revelation seriously, it fails. The "golden age" of God's redemptive history was the time of His special dealing with Israel. After some intervening dispensations, the plan of God calls for a reversion to His dealings with Israel. What is now transpiring is a sort of departure from the plan, an interim arrangement. Consequently the Old Testament has, in a sense, not really been superseded.

Second, the distinction between Israel and the church, so basic and crucial to dispensationalism, is difficult to maintain consistently. Dispensationalists have carefully selected passages that favor (or at least can accommodate) their interpretation. Other passages, however, are not so easily disposed of. In Romans 9 and Galatians 3, for example, it is difficult to escape the conclusion that Paul regarded the church, Jew and Gentile alike, as the true heir to the promises originally made to national Israel. It does appear that there will be a period of special favor toward the Jews and that they will in large numbers turn to God. It seems likely, however, that this will be brought about through their being converted and integrated into the church rather than through God resuming the relationship He had with them, as the chosen or covenant nation, in the Old Testament.

Third, the distinction between the kingdom of God and the kingdom of heaven, on which so much also depends, is difficult to maintain.[25] The passages in Mark and Luke that are parallel to Matthew 13 use the expression "kingdom of God" instead of "kingdom of heaven." Matthew alone uses the latter expression. It is difficult to believe that these two expressions designate two different entities in otherwise parallel passages. The authors seem to describe one entity with two phrases. Matthew was writing primarily to Jews, who regarded the name of Jehovah as so sacred that it should not even be pronounced. A common substitute for it was "heaven" or "the heavens." On this basis, "kingdom of heaven" was simply a nonprofane substitute for "kingdom of God" for people who had convictions against using the word. This explanation of the two phrases seems better than that of the dispensationalists. To build one's whole view of the nature of the kingdom and its recipients upon this distinction in terminology is to build on a shaky foundation.

Finally, dispensationalism is inconsistent when it abandons its extremely literal interpretation of prophecy for a virtually allegorical interpretation of historical narrative, especially when there is no warrant for this either in the immediate context of a particular passage or in another portion of Scripture. The dispensationalist seems to lose control of exegesis.

---

25. Ryrie, *Dispensationalism Today,* pp. 170–73.

Chapter 7

Pretribulationism

We come now to the discussion of the relationship of Christ's coming to the event (or series of events) known as the great tribulation. Will He return to remove His church from the world prior to the tribulation, or will the church go through the entire sequence? Or will it perhaps experience part of the tribulation and then be delivered from the world before the major (and most severe) part of it occurs?

Theoretically, tribulational views could be attached to any of the millennial positions. In practice, however, these questions have been raised and dealt with primarily by premillennialists—perhaps because premillennialists have frequently given more attention to the details of eschatology than have advocates of the other two millennial views. For purposes of this discussion, the tribulational views will be treated as subdivisions of premillennialism.

The first tribulational view we will discuss is pretribulationism. It is important first to observe the relationship between this eschatological position and the general theological system known as dispensationalism. In practice they are almost invariably wedded to one another, yet logically they are somewhat independent. All dispensationalists are pretribulationists—for pretribulationism is a part of the full system of dispensationalism—but not all pretribulationists are dispensationalists. The pretribulational rapture may be based upon independent exegetical grounds, rather than inferred from dispensational premises.

125

Overview of Pretribulationism

The beginning point for examining pretribulationism is its view of the nature of the great tribulation. Pretribulationists insist that this is indeed the *great* tribulation, a tribulation quite unequalled in all of history. While some other eschatologists emphasize that the church has always experienced persecution and hence tribulation, the pretribulationist sees this great tribulation as so intense as not to be easily confused with tribulation in general. To be sure, numerous Biblical passages speak of the tribulation and warfare that is characteristic of the saints' experience in all ages of God's redemptive dealings with His children. In sharp contrast to this, however, is the Scriptural teaching that a future period of unprecedented tribulation will overshadow all previous times of trouble. This involves three classes of people: (1) the nation of Israel, (2) the pagan Gentile world, and (3) the saints or elect who will live in that time of trouble.[1]

This great tribulation has a definite, twofold purpose: (1) to conclude "the times of the Gentiles" (Luke 21:24), and (2) to prepare for the restoration and regathering of Israel in the millennial reign of Christ following the second advent. The tribulation thus serves as a transition period in the plan of God. Pretribulationists insist most emphatically that the primary purpose of the tribulation is not to purge the church or to discipline believers.[2]

A second and extremely important feature of pretribulationism is the idea that Jesus will come for His church prior to the great tribulation to "rapture" it out of the world. The word *rapture* is derived from *rapere,* the Latin translation of "caught up" in I Thessalonians 4:17. The Greek word generally related to the rapture is παρουσία (which is transliterated *parousia*). This coming of Christ *for* the church will involve believers being caught up from the earth and meeting Christ in the air. Christ will not descend all the way to the earth, as He will in the second coming (the coming *with* the church) when He descends to the Mount of Olives. Thus, His coming will not be observed by the unbelieving world, although its effects (i.e., the absence of a substantial number of persons) will be readily discernible.[3]

---

1. John F. Walvoord, *The Rapture Question,* p. 43.
2. Ibid.   3. Ibid., pp. 101, 198.

The effect of the rapture is to remove the church from the scene of world history for the seven-year tribulation. Dispensationalism, with its sharp distinction between Israel and the church, sees the tribulation as marking the transition between God's (temporary) dealing with the church and the resumption of His primary dealing with national Israel. The "blessed hope" of the believer, then, is deliverance from this great tribulation.

At the rapture two things will happen: (1) saints who are alive will be "translated," that is, changed into the nature and condition that will be theirs for all eternity; and (2) believers who have died in Christ will be resurrected to join the translated living believers in heaven (the "old" heaven). This is how pretribulationists interpret I Thessalonians 4.[4]

At this time all Christians will be judged (II Cor. 5:10). They will appear before the judgment seat of Christ and be judged according to their works. This judgment will not extend to all persons who have ever lived, or even to all who will ultimately be saved. It relates only to "we all," which is believers in Christ during the present age (i.e., the church). This judgment will not separate the saved from the unsaved; it will reward the good works of the persons being judged.[5]

At the end of this seven-year period during which the church, having received its reward, is with Christ in heaven and non-Christians are experiencing great tribulation on earth, Jesus will return with the church in triumph. This great event will be visible to all. It will be accompanied by a second resurrection: a resurrection of believers who have died during the tribulation. They then share in the millennial reign with Christ and the other believers.[6]

The second coming, then, has two stages or phases. In the first phase Christ comes *for* the church, to remove it from the world. In the second phase He comes *with* the church, to set up the earthly kingdom, establish His rule, and initiate the millennium. In the posttribulational view, as we shall see later, these are two aspects of a single event or occurrence. Posttribulationism discerns only two

---

4. Walvoord, *The Return of the Lord*, p. 55.

5. Ibid., p. 116.

6. Charles L. Feinberg, *Premillennialism or Amillennialism? The Premillennial and Amillennial Systems of Interpretation Analyzed and Compared*, p. 146.

resurrections, while pretribulationism sees three (the resurrection of the righteous dead at the rapture just prior to the tribulation, the resurrection just after the tribulation of saints who have died during the tribulation, and the resurrection of unbelievers at the end of the millennium). Because posttribulationism does not divide the coming of Christ into two stages, it does not distinguish between the first two of these resurrections.

A crucial tenet of pretribulationism is the doctrine of imminence,[7] according to which the return of Christ (the rapture or the parousia) may occur *at any time.* No further events must occur, no additional prophecies must be fulfilled, before the rapture. This of course is closely tied to the concept of pretribulationism. If the second coming were a unitary or unified event, it could not occur at any moment; the great tribulation would have to take place first. But in fact Christ can come at any time, even before this sentence is completed. Pretribulationists see this belief in imminency as a great incentive to urgency in Christian service. Because we do not know when our opportunity for labor will be over, we are more intent to use the present time well.

History of Pretribulationism

In the chapter on premillennialism, we noted that chiliasm was a dominant force in the early centuries of the Christian era. Yet when we examine closely this chiliasm, we scarcely find it to be the pretribulational form that we are examining in this chapter. Rather than anticipating a deliverance from the tribulation that was to come, the early Christians evidently expected to experience that great affliction personally.

The Didache, written in the first quarter of the second century, was apparently intended in part to prepare Christians for the coming hardship. The last chapter reads as follows:

> 1. "Watch" over your life: "let your lamps" be not quenched "and your loins" be not ungirded, but be "ready," for ye know not "the hour in which our Lord cometh." 2. But be frequently gathered together seeking the things which are profitable for your souls, for the whole time of your faith shall not profit you except ye be found perfect at the last

---

7. Walvoord, *The Rapture Question,* pp. 75–82.

time; 3. for in the last days the false prophets and the corrupters shall be multiplied, and the sheep shall be turned into wolves, and love shall change to hate; 4. for as lawlessness increaseth they shall hate one another and persecute and betray, and then shall appear the deceiver of the world as a Son of God, and shall do signs and wonders and the earth shall be given over into his hands and he shall commit iniquities which have never been since the world began. 5. Then shall the creation of mankind come to the fiery trial and "many shall be offended" and be lost, but "they who endure" in their faith "shall be saved" by the curse itself. 6. And "then shall appear the signs" of the truth. First the sign spread out in Heaven, then the sign of the sound of the trumpet, and thirdly the resurrection of the dead: 7. but not of all the dead, but as it was said, "The Lord shall come and all his saints with him." 8. Then shall the world "see the Lord coming on the clouds of Heaven."[8]

Verse 5 suggests that believers will be present in this tribulation and will by their endurance demonstrate the reality of their faith. It also says that all created men will be tried by fire, with many being offended and perishing. Only verse 7 admits of a possible pretribulational understanding—the reference to all the saints coming with the Lord is faintly reminiscent of the pretribulational "coming with" the church, as contrasted with the "coming for" the church.

Other early writings are similarly premillennial without being pretribulational. Two examples are the Epistle of Barnabas and the Shepherd of Hermas. The latter contains a passage that sometimes is cited as an instance of belief in a pretribulational rapture, but closer examination of it reveals that it is not.[9]

Perhaps the first of the church fathers to give a detailed treatment of the tribulation was Irenaeus (130?–200?). His writings reveal that he was a thoroughgoing premillennialist but did not believe in a pretribulational rapture. Rather, he saw Christ coming at the end of the tribulation to destroy the Antichrist and to deliver His church.

---

8. In *The Apostolic Fathers,* trans. Kirsopp Lake, 2 vols. (Cambridge: Harvard University, 1959–1965), 1:333.

9. George E. Ladd, *The Blessed Hope,* p. 23.

But when this Antichrist shall have devastated all things in this world, he will reign for three years and six months, and sit in the temple at Jerusalem; and then the Lord will come from heaven in the clouds, in the glory of the Father, sending this man [Antichrist] and those who follow him into the lake of fire; but bringing in for the righteous [the Church] the times of the kingdom.[10]

For all these and other words were unquestionably spoken in reference to the resurrection of the just, which takes place after the coming of the Antichrist, and the destruction of all nations under his rule; in [the times of] which [resurrection] the righteous shall reign in the earth, waxing stronger by the sight of the Lord: and through Him they shall become accustomed to partake in the glory of God the Father, and shall enjoy in the kingdom intercourse and communion with the holy angels, and union with spiritual beings; and [with respect to] those whom the Lord shall find in the flesh, awaiting Him from heaven, and who have suffered tribulation, as well as escaped the hands of the Wicked one.[11]

Pretribulationists generally concede that there is no complete statement of pretribulationism in the writings of the early fathers. But, as John F. Walvoord said, neither is there in their writings a detailed and established exposition of any other feature of premillennialism.[12] Indeed, he noted, most important doctrines were developed over a period of several centuries. The doctrine of the Trinity did not receive final and settled statement until the fourth century and thereafter, beginning with the Council of Nicaea in 325. The doctrine of human depravity was not a settled doctrine of the church until the fifth century and after. And the doctrine of the priesthood of the believer was not established until the Protestant Reformation. If these doctrines, basic and central as they are, were not formulated definitively overnight, is it any wonder that the details of eschatology, which are especially difficult, have been slow in unfolding?

---

10. *Against Heresies* 30.4, trans. Alexander Roberts and James Donaldson, in *The Ante-Nicene Fathers,* ed. Roberts and Donaldson, 10 vols. (Buffalo: Christian Literature, 1885–1896), 1:560.

11. Ibid. 35.1, p. 565.

12. *The Rapture Question,* pp. 52–53.

Nonetheless, it is true that these early Christian writings contain a belief in imminency, which Walvoord maintains is the central feature of pretribulationism. The early church did not face all the problems raised by the doctrine of imminency, such as its relation to the tribulation. Whether the expectation was of an any-moment coming, as it is on the part of modern pretribulationists, is debatable. The early church seems rather to have expected that a whole set of events was soon to occur, including the tribulation.[13]

While there are in the writings of the early fathers seeds from which the doctrine of the pretribulational rapture could be developed, it is difficult to find in them an unequivocal statement of the type of imminency usually believed in by pretribulationists. And there are in these writings some clearly posttribulational expressions, as even Walvoord has conceded:

> The expectancy of the Lord's coming was clouded, however, by the belief that the events of the tribulation were impending, and that Christ's coming to establish His kingdom was posttribulational. While all of the early fathers are not clear on the question, some of them were posttribulational. Pretribulationists usually concede that none of them taught the precise interpretation of Darby.[14]

During the Middle Ages, as we have seen, the eschatological interpretation gradually adopted was the so-called historical view, which places eschatological events within the history of the church. In the Reformation, Protestants tended to identify the Antichrist with papal Rome. The tribulation was already occurring, or would occur within the customary span of history. In this framework there was certainly no expectation of an imminent coming. Even Protestants who were premillennial tended to follow the historical mode of interpretation.

In the early nineteenth century clear-cut pretribulationism arose in the views of John Nelson Darby (1800–1882), a member of the Plymouth Brethren movement. This movement began in Dublin in 1825 as a group of men concerned about the spiritual condition of the Protestant church in Ireland. Similar prayer- and fellowship-groups sprang up elsewhere. Darby, who entered the fellowship in

---

13. Ladd, *The Blessed Hope*, p. 20.
14. *The Rapture Question*, p. 54.

1827, and other leaders of the movement became involved in prophetic conferences carried on at Powerscourt House. The view expounded there was much like that found in the early church: a futuristic view of the coming of the Antichrist, who will inflict severe persecution upon the church during the great tribulation. According to this view Christ will return at the end of the tribulation to deliver His church.[15] Darby introduced a modification of this view: Christ will come to rapture the church before the tribulation and before He comes in glory to establish the millennial kingdom.[16]

Darby's view resulted in a division within the Brethren movement. Samuel P. Tregelles, a member of the Brethren in the movement's early days, claimed that the idea of a secret coming of Christ to rapture the church originated in an utterance at the church of Edward Irving, a preacher at the prophetic conference from which the Powerscourt House meetings derived. Darby took this as the voice of the Spirit and accepted it as doctrine, but Tregelles, Benjamin W. Newton, and other leaders who held to a posttribulational perspective rejected it. Contention within the Brethren movement was the result.[17]

Darby visited the United States no fewer than six times between 1859 and 1874 and expounded his views of eschatology. To many Americans Darbyism constituted the recovery of the Biblical doctrine of the glorious second coming of Christ.[18]

Interest in prophetic teaching and preaching was a major factor in the rise of the Bible Conference movement, in which ministers and laymen who accepted a set of commonly accepted beliefs gathered for fellowship. The best known conference was the Niagara Conference. After it was discontinued, a new conference was established at Seacliff, Long Island, in 1901. It was at Seacliff that C. I. Scofield (1843–1921) conceived the idea of a reference Bible. While many of the early leaders of these conferences were

---

15. Ladd, *The Blessed Hope*, pp. 36–41; Clarence B. Bass, *Backgrounds to Dispensationalism: Its Historical Genesis and Ecclesiastical Implications*, pp. 67–68.

16. Ladd, *The Blessed Hope*, p. 37.

17. Ibid., p. 41.

18. Ibid., p. 43.

posttribulationists, the majority were pretribulationists, and it was they who made the greatest impact upon the movement.[19] The Scofield Reference Bible was particularly effective in spreading pretribulationism. Widely distributed in conservative circles, it was the only Bible study aid possessed by many laymen. Also effective in promoting pretribulationism was the Bible institute movement. As more and more seminaries of the major denominations turned toward a liberal theology, conservative churches increasingly looked to the Bible institutes for pastors, and these institutes were almost exclusively pretribulational. As a result this viewpoint was adopted by most conservative independent and Baptist churches, as well as by many other "free churches."

Tenets of Pretribulationism

We come now to a closer examination of the major tenets of pretribulationism and of the arguments advanced in their support. We will look at the issues of pretribulationism per se, rather than at the broader system of dispensational interpretation within which it frequently is found. There are three considerations here: the church appears to be absent during the tribulation; the church is removed prior to the tribulation; and the Lord's coming is imminent. We will examine these in turn.

The Church's Absence During the Tribulation

The first consideration involves a definite conception of the nature of the church. It is here that pretribulationism's close connection with dispensationalism first becomes apparent. It is true, says the pretribulationist, that there will be believers or saints or elect present during the tribulation. Indeed, Matthew says that for the sake of the elect those days will be shortened. The posttribulationist makes a serious mistake in assuming that these saints are the church. This mistake in turn rests upon an even larger error: equating or identifying the church with all believers during all periods of God's dealing with mankind.[20]

---

19. Ibid., p. 44.
20. Walvoord, *The Rapture Question,* pp. 62–63.

Posttribulationists have claimed that a rapture of the church at the conclusion of the tribulation is affirmed in Matthew 24:31: "And he shall send forth his angels with a great sound of a trumpet, and they shall gather together his elect from the four winds, from one end of heaven to the other." This passage and others like it, however, at no point utilize the distinctive expressions *church* or *body of Christ* or any other term that clearly and peculiarly refers to the church. It always uses the more general term *elect*.[21] If the church were involved, would that not be made explicit and clear? Walvoord suggested that the context of Matthew 24 limits the word *elect* to one of two meanings: the living saints on the earth at the time of the second advent (cf. Matt. 24:22) or Israel as an elect nation. Similarly the words *church* and *churches* do not appear in Revelation after chapter 3 (except in 22:16, where the ascended Christ declares that He is sending a message to the churches that are on earth when Revelation is being written).

But even if the broader meaning of *elect* applies in Matthew 24:31, it is still quite possible to harmonize the passage with pretribulationism. Matthew speaks of the elect being gathered "from the four winds, from one end of heaven to the other"; Mark, of their being gathered "from the uttermost part of the earth to the uttermost part of heaven" (Mark 13:27). To be sure, at the second advent the church, raptured prior to the tribulation, will be gathered from heaven; the Old Testament saints will be resurrected; and the elect on earth will be gathered. Walvoord concluded that while this passage does not prove pretribulationism, "it does not offer any evidence whatever against it."[22]

But what of the elect who are present during this great tribulation? If they are not the church, who are they? Certainly a remnant of godly believers will be present when Christ returns to establish His kingdom. Revelation 7:4 speaks of 144,000 of all the tribes of Israel. These are not the church, for members of the church are not called "the children of Israel." While members of the church are referred to as children of Abraham, "the father of us all" (Rom. 4:16), that is quite different from the designation

---

21. Ibid., p. 63.
22. Ibid.

"children of Israel." These 144,000 sealed servants of God are Jews.[23] In addition, Revelation 7:9 speaks of a great multitude that includes a large number of Gentiles who become believers during the tribulation through the faithful witness of the Jews. These two groups retain their national characteristics as saved Gentiles and saved Jews. None of the special and peculiar promises given to the church in the present age is given to these saints of the tribulation.[24]

The Church's Removal from the World

Gordon Lewis took the argument one step further and contended that the passages we have just considered actually support a pretribulational rapture of the church; they refer, he pointed out, only to the Jews. Note the context of Matthew 24. The disciples had asked the Lord for a sign of His coming and of the end of the age. This question, like the one in Acts 1:6 ("Lord, will you at this time restore the kingdom to Israel?") was asked within the frame of reference of Jewish concerns, and Christ's answer was in terms of the Jews' future. It is Jews who are pictured as present during the tribulation. To take the passage out of its context and apply it to all believers is to do violence to Scripture. When seen in this light, the interpretation of the passage becomes easier. After the initial signs the Jews will see in the temple the desolating sacrilege spoken of by Daniel the prophet. The time of Jacob's trouble will be shortened for the sake of the elect (Israelites). Following the tribulation the Son of man of whom Daniel spoke will come in the clouds of heaven and gather His elect. Jesus' statement that this generation would not pass away until all of these signs were fulfilled was a promise that the Jewish race would not disappear until all of these events pertaining to its restoration occurred.[25]

Some would reply, however, that this Jewish emphasis is merely "clothing" for Matthew, who wrote for Jewish readers. But Mark and Luke maintain these Jewish features, and the latter even adds

---

23. E. Schuyler English, *Re-Thinking the Rapture: An Examination of What the Scriptures Teach as to the Time of the Translation of the Church in Relation to the Tribulation,* pp. 100–101.

24. Ibid., p. 103; Walvoord, *The Rapture Question,* pp. 68–69.

25. "Biblical Evidence for Pretribulationism," p. 220.

some: Jerusalem will be surrounded by armies (21:20) and will be "trodden down by the Gentiles" until the times of the Gentiles are fulfilled (21:24). Thus, the Jewish emphasis in the Olivet discourse is not incidental but intrinsic, for the elect in the tribulation are elect Jews.[26]

The preceding argument is basically a negative one, an argument from silence. In addition, however, the pretribulationist finds definite statements and promises that the church will not be in the world during the great tribulation. Several of these are in Paul's two letters to the Thessalonians.

Paul described for the Thessalonians the great wrath to come, and he promised that they would not undergo these severe afflictions: "For God has not destined us for wrath, but to obtain salvation through our Lord Jesus Christ" (I Thess. 5:9); and Jesus "delivers us from the wrath to come" (I Thess. 1:9–10). Luke 21:36 certainly seems to refer as well to an escape from the coming day of trial: "But watch at all times, praying that you may have strength to escape all these things that will take place, and to stand before the Son of man."[27]

The pattern of events surrounding the tribulation, according to Paul in I Thessalonians, is as follows: the living dead will be resurrected and the living will be raptured at the coming of the Lord (4:15–17); the rapture will come suddenly, like a child being born (5:3) or a thief coming in the night, removing the church from the sphere where the tribulation occurs. Many will be lulled into a false security. Believers, however, are not to be in a sleepy or drunken stupor, but alert and sober (5:8). If they are alert, wrath will not come upon them.[28]

Posttribulationists maintain that the promise is for protection from the wrath of God, not for removal from the scene. Pretribulationists reject this as inadequate. Lewis said: "If a posttribulationist imports into this context a theory of preservation from divine wrath by some other means during the tribulation, he ought to produce some evidence from the context for his theory."[29] Other

26. Ibid.
27. Ibid., pp. 222–25.
28. Ibid., p. 216.
29. Ibid.

Scripture portions, pretribulationists argue, affirm that believers are kept or delivered *from* the wrath of God, not preserved within it.[30] Revelation 3:10 says, "I will keep you *from* the hour of trial which is coming on the whole world, to try those who dwell upon the earth." Romans 5:9 says, "Since, therefore, we are now justified by his blood, much more shall we be saved by him from the wrath of God." The illustration in II Peter 2:6–9, the deliverance of Lot from Sodom, suggests deliverance out of or away from God's wrath. The same is true of Noah and his family, delivered from the flood by the ark, as well as of Rahab at Jericho. These examples, although not conclusive proof, confirm the idea that God characteristically delivers believers from wrath designed to judge unbelievers. They suggest that God's deliverance of His people from tribulation will be in keeping with this general principle.[31]

II Thessalonians also presents an interesting commentary upon the tribulation and the rapture. Some Thessalonian Christians were afraid that the day of Christ had already been "present" (2:2). ("Present" is a more accurate rendering than "at hand," and it does not conflict with Paul's earlier teaching that the day was in fact "at hand.") These Christians were concerned about Christ's return in flaming fire, taking vengeance upon the ungodly (1:7–9). Paul sought to ease their minds by pointing out that before this day of the Lord's vengeance comes, certain other events must occur: the "departure" (ἀποστασία) and the revealing of the man of sin (Antichrist). A restrainer now prevents the Antichrist from appearing (2:7), but when this restrainer is removed, the wicked one will be revealed (2:8). Lewis insisted that the "departure" (2:4) and the removal of the restrainer (2:7) are the same event.[32]

Usually the Greek noun ἀποστασία is rendered by its transliteration, *apostasy*, and if it is so rendered here, it means "a moral, spiritual, or doctrinal abandonment of the faith." E. Schuyler English, however, has propounded what Walvoord calls a "somewhat novel" interpretation of II Thessalonians 2:3, and Lewis has

---

30. English, *Re-Thinking the Rapture,* p. 89.

31. Walvoord, *The Rapture Question,* pp. 70–71.

32. "Biblical Evidence for Pretribulationism," p. 217.

adopted and defended it:[33] ἀποστασία in 2:3 should be translated "departure" rather than "apostasy," and it refers to the rapture of the church out of the world prior to the tribulation.

It is true, these men noted, that the most common and primary meanings of ἀποστασία are "defection," "revolt," or "rebellion" against God. But, there are also secondary connotations, that of "disappearance" or "departure."[34] To ascertain the meaning of a word, one must first ascertain its customary usage in the New Testament. In only one other instance (in Acts 21:21, where the concept is to "forsake Moses") does ἀποστασία allude with certainty to rebellion against God. The word also occurs six times in the Septuagint. While it always connotes a departure from God, in each case either a descriptive phrase or the context requires that this be the meaning. Although the noun is rare in the New Testament, the verb from which it is derived (ἀφίστημι) is used fifteen times. In only three instances does it refer to religious departure, and each time this meaning is indicated either by a descriptive phrase ("from the faith"—I Tim. 4:1; cf. Heb. 3:12) or by the context (Luke 8:13). In the other cases, ἀφίστημι means "to depart," whether from a person (Acts 12:10; Luke 4:13), from iniquity (II Tim. 2:19), from the temple (Luke 2:37), or from the body (II Cor. 12:8). English and Lewis concluded that "departure" is a legitimate translation of ἀποστασία in the New Testament and that it is the correct rendering of the word in II Thessalonians 2:4. Thus, Paul was affirming and asserting a pretribulational rapture.[35]

Christ's Imminent Return

The third main tenet is that of imminency. Because the church will be raptured or translated before the tribulation, neither the tribulation nor any other events predicted in Scripture need to be fulfilled before Christ comes. Christ can come for the church

---

33. English, *Re-Thinking the Rapture,* pp. 68–70; Walvoord, *The Rapture Question,* pp. 71–72; Lewis, "Biblical Evidence for Pretribulationism," pp. 217–19.

34. H. G. Liddell and Robert Scott, *A Greek-English Lexicon,* 9th ed. (New York: Oxford, 1940).

35. *Re-Thinking the Rapture,* pp. 67–69; "Biblical Evidence for Pretribulationism," pp. 217–18.

literally *at any moment*. This belief is usually supported by several lines of argument.

The first is the passages urging believers to be watchful because they do not know the time of Christ's coming. These passages are found in both the Gospels and the Epistles.

In Matthew 24 and 25, even after listing many prior signs of His return, Christ urged His disciples to be ever ready for His coming. The day and hour of His return are known only to the Father. Because the return of Christ will be as unexpected as the flood was in Noah's time, the servants of the Lord are to occupy themselves, using and investing the talents the Lord has given them. Jesus even stated explicitly that not only did they not know the times and seasons, but it was not for them to know, implying that they were not to inquire about this.[36]

These teachings suggest that the coming of Christ could occur at any moment. If events such as the tribulation must first come to pass, the point of saying "You do not know the time" is difficult to see.

The teaching of the Gospels, especially of Jesus' great eschatological discourse, is also the message of the epistles. In view of the fact that the time of the Lord's coming is unknown and that His coming is surely near, numerous passages urge watchfulness. We are to await eagerly the redemption of the body (Rom. 8:19–25) and the revealing of the Lord Jesus (I Cor. 1:7). We await our Savior from heaven (Phil. 4:5). We renounce worldliness and live godly lives, awaiting the blessed hope of Christ's appearing (Titus 2:13). We are to be patient, for the coming of the Lord is at hand (James 5:8). We should not grumble against our brethren because "the Judge is standing at the doors" (James 5:9). We are to keep ourselves in the love of God, waiting "for the mercy of our Lord Jesus Christ unto eternal life" (Jude 21).[37]

All of these texts argue that the coming of the Lord can be at any moment. A final argument for imminency is that there can be a blessed *hope* only if it is the Lord for whom we look. If the next event in God's plan is the coming of the evil one (Antichrist) and of tribulation, we scarcely have a basis for hope. Fear and appre-

---

36. Lewis, "Biblical Evidence for Pretribulationism," p. 222.

37. Ibid., pp. 222–23.

hensiveness would be more appropriate. Paul's exhortation to comfort one another with the hope of Christ's coming (I Thess. 4:18) certainly implies that the prospect for the church is something other than persecution, suffering, probable martyrdom and destruction. The whole point of the passage in I Thessalonians hangs on the Lord's coming being imminent and pretribulational.[38]

Evaluation of Pretribulationism

Positive Aspects

Pretribulationism, through its concept of any-moment imminency, imparts a sense of expectancy to the Christian faith. The early church looked forward to the coming of the Lord as a reality by which they could govern their lives. This became a *purifying* hope. Pretribulationism has managed to recapture something of this first-century ethos. It has also given to the task of the church a dimension of urgency. If the time we have in which to do the work of Christ is limited, and if the end to this period of opportunity can come at any moment, it is imperative to do the work as quickly as possible. An aggressive approach to the mission of the church is the logical consequence.

Pretribulationists have kept the discussion of eschatology alive at times when others have not. In recent years we have seen a tremendous revival of interest in eschatology. We might even term our age "paneschatological." Pretribulationists have anticipated this revival of interest within the broader theological landscape.

Finally, they have been alert to the eschatological dimensions of the whole of Scripture. While it may be true that occasionally pretribulationists have found more eschatology in the Bible than is actually there, they have called the attention of others to the eschatological significance of passages that perhaps would otherwise have been overlooked. In particular, some secondary emphases and applications have been overlooked by those who have considered only the primary or most obvious meaning.

---

38. Walvoord, *The Return of the Lord,* p. 51.

Negative Aspects

The first defect in pretribulationism lies in the weakness of its evidence for the concept of any-moment imminence. Some of the Scriptures to which pretribulationists appeal do not seem to support this idea.

The basic argument for imminency is the numerous injunctions in Scripture to watch for Christ's coming and the warnings that His coming will occur at an unlikely time and without recognizable antecedents. These injunctions are warranted, argues the pretribulationist, only if the rapture can happen at any time. If there are unfulfilled events that must come to pass before the rapture, there is no point to such watchfulness.

But does this follow? Why do the entreaty to watch for Christ's coming and the warning that the time of His coming is unknown require the conclusion that He could come at any moment? Could it not be simply that the number, nature, and duration of the intervening events are unknown? To put it another way, it may be that there is necessarily a time interval but that we do not know its extent.

Further, it appears that when the "watch" and the "you do not know the time" passages were written, they could not possibly have meant an any-moment imminency. For one thing, Jesus indicated to the early disciples that His coming would be delayed for some time. This seems to be the teaching of at least three of His parables: the nobleman who went to a far country (Luke 19:11–27), the wise and foolish virgins (see Matt. 25:5), and the talents (Matt. 25:19).

The parable of the servants presupposes a period of delay during which the genuineness of the servants can be established (Luke 12:41–48; Matt. 24:45–51). When the master delayed his return, the false servant became lackadaisical and the true servant continued to wait and watch faithfully. Walvoord, recognizing this feature of the parables, suggested that the long period of delay would be satisfied by "a few years."[39] Yet such a delay is all that posttribulationism requires.

---

39. "Premillennialism and the Tribulation," p. 2.

At the time Jesus spoke these words, there were also certain events which, it would seem, had to transpire before His second coming: for example, Peter had to grow old and become infirm (John 21:12ff.); the gospel had to be preached to all the nations (even before Christ comes "for" the church); and possibly Jerusalem had to fall before Christ's second coming.

Pretribulationists sometimes reply that when the statements were made, they could not mean that the coming was imminent, for these intervening events still had to transpire. Now that they have been fulfilled, however, the coming is imminent. The problem, however, is deeper than that. If at the time the words were first spoken and heard they did not require the concept of imminence, then the words do not require imminence at present either. The passage of a few years does not and cannot invest language with meaning that it did not previously have. The pretribulationist may argue that the words should be understood as meaning, for example, "The Lord may come at any time, *unless* Peter has not yet grown old." This, however, is just the point. There is no reason why additional exceptions may not be added to the list, such as, "The Lord may come at any time, *unless* the great tribulation has not yet occurred."

The other major problem for pretribulationism concerns the Biblical passages in which they see descriptions of the rapture (the coming *for* the church). One is I Thessalonians 4:16–17. While the rapture (in which the Lord does not come all the way to earth) is supposed to be relatively inconspicuous, not seen by unbelievers, its description ("with a cry of command, with the archangel's call, and with the sound of the trumpet of God") makes it sound like something unmistakable. The suggestion of posttribulationists that this refers not to a "coming for" the church but to a single, second advent of Christ seems to fit the description better.

Further difficulty arises in connection with the reference in II Thessalonians 2:3 to ἀποστασία. While it is true that "departure" is a possible translation, is it the best possible translation? In the context nothing seems to suggest a departure (or "rapture") of believers. A safe rule of interpretation is to adopt the most common or most likely meaning of a term unless there is some good reason in the context for adopting another. Since the context speaks of the man of sin and of the lawlessness and unrighteousness that will accompany his appearance, it seems most reasonable to render ἀποστασία in the usual sense of "apostasy" or "departure from the faith."

Chapter 8

Posttribulationism

Posttribulationism, like pretribulationism, is primarily a subdivision of premillennialism. Technically all nonpremillennialists are posttribulationists. Few nonpremillennialists, however, concern themselves with the idea of a tribulation. Thus we may safely limit our treatment of posttribulationism to posttribulationists of the premillennial variety.

Overview of Posttribulationism

The first major feature of posttribulationism is of course that the church will not be removed from the world prior to the tribulation but will go through it, enduring it by the grace and strength of God. Only after that great and terrible period will Christ come.[1] Posttribulationists do not believe that the rapture will follow the tribulation, for they do not use the terms *rapture* and *translation* (neither of which is a Biblical term). It is not that the posttribulationist desires to endure the tribulation—nothing could be further from his wishes—but that he finds no evidence in the Bible for this sort of deliverance from the great affliction that is to come.

Often the pretribulationist argues that the church will surely not be exposed to God's wrath. This the posttribulationist readily concedes; in fact he insists upon the point. The posttribulationist frequently distinguishes between the great tribulation and the wrath of God. The tribulation, which is in part inflicted by non-Christians

---

1. George E. Ladd, *The Blessed Hope*, p. 88.

and the devil, will be experienced by all who are alive and on earth at the time. The wrath of God will overlap with the tribulation, but it is intended only for the wicked; the saints of God will be spared from it.

At the end of the tribulation, Christ will come the second time. This is the hope of the Christian. Implicit in this belief is the concept that the return of the Lord will be a unitary event.[2] It will not have two stages or two phases—a coming *for* and a coming *with* the church. All passages that refer to a coming of the Lord refer to this single event. This coming will conclude the period of great tribulation, establish the kingdom of God on earth, and usher in the millennial period. While the term *rapture* is seldom if ever used by posttribulationists, what the term usually designates will indeed happen at the end of the tribulation. When Christ comes, the saints who have died will be resurrected. They, together with the saints who are alive, will be caught up to meet the Lord and then return to earth to reign with Him.

For the posttribulationist, then, there are only two resurrections: one of all the righteous dead at the beginning of the millennium, and one of all the rest (the unrighteous) at the end of the millennium. Because there is no interlude between the coming *for* the church and the coming *with* the church, no saints die during the interlude and there is no need for another resurrection of the righteous.[3]

The posttribulationist is generally less literal in his approach to the last things than is the pretribulationist. This shows itself in several ways. The posttribulationist is not sure that the tribulation will be precisely seven calendar years. The reference in Daniel is to seventy "sevens," which have been understood by many to be weeks, and weeks of years, rather than days. Passages that describe the tribulation itself do not specify its length. The posttribulationist is also unsure about the length of the millennium. What the posttribulationist *is* certain about is that for an extended period of time the Lord will personally rule upon the earth.

Further, the posttribulationist does not find in Scripture quite the detailed picture of the millennium that the pretribulationist

---

2. Ibid., p. 70.
3. Ibid., p. 82.

does. The latter sees many Old Testament prophetic passages being fulfilled in the millennium; the posttribulationist does not see the millennium as a great repository of prophetic fulfillment.

The ethos of posttribulationism is therefore quite different from that of pretribulationism, being in many ways more like that of amillennialism. Should a pretribulationist decide that there is insufficient Biblical evidence for a millennium, it would demand a rather major alteration of his whole eschatological system. It would require a considerably less radical adjustment for most posttribulationists, however. The millennium, in other words, plays a much less crucial role in their theology.

In the posttribulational scheme, there are signs or indications of the nearness of the Lord's coming—in particular, the great tribulation. One might expect posttribulationists, then, to be date-setters, but they are just the opposite. Because the length of the tribulation is not certain, no schedule or timetable is possible.

This affects the idea of imminency as well. Many posttribulationists use the adjective *imminent* of the second coming, but the vast preponderance of posttribulationists mean by this not that Christ's coming can occur at *any moment* but that it is *impending*. The sequence of events that includes the coming of the Lord may well be at hand. It is this complex of events that is imminent, not one specific event.[4]

The posttribulationist has a hope, but it is not for a deliverance from the coming tribulation. Some pretribulationists assert that the appearing of the man of sin is no basis for hope. The posttribulationist affirms, however, that his hope is that no matter what may occur, the Lord will come and bring all of it to an end. His hope is in the Lord's *second coming*.[5]

The references to the elect who are present in the midst of the tribulation are, the posttribulationist believes, the church, not elect Jews. This points up another feature of the theology of most posttribulationists: there is no sharp distinction between Israel and the church. While Israel will probably have a special place in the last times, it will be not because God reverts to dealing with Israel as in

---

4. Robert H. Gundry, *The Church and the Tribulation,* pp. 29–43.

5. Ladd, *The Blessed Hope,* p. 13.

older times, but because He will incorporate an unusually large number of Jews into the church.[6]

The church has replaced national Israel as God's covenant people, according to posttribulationism.[7] Paul stated in Galatians 3 that those who have the *faith* of Abraham, rather than the *blood* of Abraham, are the true sons of Abraham. Rather than being totally unforeseen in Old Testament prophecies, as some pretribulationists claim, the church fulfills many of those prophecies and promises. Some posttribulationists understand the church to include all believers at all times and places. To restrict "the elect" in the tribulation to certain literal or national Jews is therefore inconceivable.

Posttribulationism combines elements from two other views into its understanding of the kingdom of God. Like postmillennialism it sees the kingdom as being present on earth or within the hearts of men, and as being within time. Like pretribulational premillennialism it sees the kingdom as being otherworldly and future. The kingdom is not growing and spreading gradually; it will come dramatically when the Lord returns.

For the posttribulationist the kingdom is both present and future.[8] Βασιλεία means basically "the *reign* of God," not "a realm" over which He is sovereign.[9] Consequently it is already present; He reigns in the hearts of all who believe in Him and obey Him. Jesus said, ". . . the kingdom of heaven is at hand" (Matt. 4:17). It will be fully realized, however, primarily in the future. Only when Christ returns will every knee bow and every tongue confess Him as Lord. In the judgment of the posttribulationist, it is important not to neglect either aspect of the kingdom in favor of the other.

History of Posttribulationism

In the preceding chapter we noted that although there was a strong premillenarian (or chiliast) strain in early Christian theology, there was no hope for a rapture prior to the tribulation. Rather, the expectation of the coming of Christ included the events pre-

---

6. Ladd, "Israel and the Church," pp. 210–13.

7. Ibid., p. 207.

8. Ladd, "Kingdom of God—Reign or Realm?," pp. 236–38.

9. Ibid., pp. 230–38.

ceding and attending His coming. There certainly was an anticipation that this complex of events would soon occur, but the expectation was for the whole set of happenings—the coming of Antichrist, the great tribulation, and the return of Christ. Let us elaborate somewhat further this viewpoint of the early church, as well as the later history of posttribulationism.

The author of the Epistle of Barnabas could not have expected Christ to return at any moment for he expected first a great final time of trouble. He warned believers to flee from the works of evil, to hate the present era, and to seek earnestly that which is able to save them. The church will go through the tribulation, and Christ will return to destroy Antichrist only at its termination. In particular, the author of the Epistle of Barnabas believed that the end would not come until the Roman Empire had been divided into ten kingdoms. This obviously could not happen at once, for at that time Rome's power was at its peak.[10]

Justin Martyr (100?–165?), one of the earliest fathers who was clearly premillennial, envisioned believers suffering great persecution and torment prior to the coming of the Lord. His reference to Antichrist, though brief, is sufficient to indicate that Justin believed that those upon whom this evil one would inflict his cruelty included the church. Justin believed that the sufferings Antichrist would inflict upon believers would not be much more severe than what Christians were already suffering for their faith.[11] In a sense, then, the great tribulation would be only an extension and intensification of what was already present. Justin himself became a martyr for his commitment to Christ.

Tertullian (160?–230?) was an avowed premillennialist, clearly anticipating the establishment of a kingdom of Christ upon the earth. In one passage he sounds as if he believed in an any-moment coming of Christ: "But what a spectacle is that fast-approaching advent of our Lord, now owned by all, now highly exalted, now a triumphant One!"[12] He cannot be considered a pretribulationist,

---

10. 4:3–4; 15:5.

11. *Dialogue with Trypho* 110.

12. *The Shows* 30, trans. S. Thelwall, in *The Ante-Nicene Fathers*, ed. Alexander Roberts and James Donaldson, 10 vols. (Buffalo: Christian Literature, 1885–1896), 3:91.

however. He did not believe that the end could come at any time; it would be preceded and announced by signs of warning. He urged his readers to pray for deliverance from the things to come. Tertullian's hope and prayers were not for the Lord to come and remove him from the tribulation, but for him to stand before the Son of man *after* a series of cosmic signs have appeared and "all of these things have taken place."[13]

Lactantius (250?–320?) discussed the last times in some detail. In one passage he said the prophets had "foretold signs by which the consummation of the times is to be expected by us from day to day, and to be feared."[14] This might sound like a belief in an any-moment coming. Upon closer examination, however, it is evident that what he constantly expected was not the coming of Christ but the occurrence of a series of signs preceding His coming. Lactantius followed the historical interpretation, seeing human history as spanning six thousand years and being followed by another thousand years, the millennium. He believed that of the six thousand years, all but two hundred fifty had transpired. During the remaining years, some major changes would have to take place. The Roman Empire must fall and government return to Asia, for the East must again rule the entire world.[15]

Lactantius vividly described the horrible conditions that will prevail in the last times. So severe will the tribulation be that it will destroy nine-tenths of the human race. The church as well as the world will suffer these evils of the end times. Antichrist will come and persecute the righteous during the last 3½ years. A special sign will herald the coming of Christ: "There shall suddenly fall from heaven a sword, that the righteous may know that the leader of the sacred warfare is about to descend." All of these considerations point to Lactantius being a posttribulationist.[16]

Hippolytus (d. 236?), bishop of Rome in the first part of the third century, wrote a treatise on the Antichrist. He interpreted

---

13. *On the Resurrection of the Flesh* 22, trans. Holmes, in *The Ante-Nicene Fathers,* 3:560–61.

14. *The Divine Institutes* 7:25, trans. William Fletcher, in *The Ante-Nicene Fathers,* 7:220.

15. Ibid., 7:25, 15, in 7:220, 212–13.

16. Ibid., 7:16–17, 19, in 7:213–16.

Revelation 12 as teaching that the adversary will persecute the church. He definitely identified the "saints" in Revelation 12 as the church. Jesus Christ will come from heaven only after the abomination of desolation is set up and all of the accompanying events transpire.[17]

George E. Ladd summarized the patristic period with apparent accuracy:

> Every church father who deals with the subject expects the Church to suffer at the hands of Antichrist. God would purify the Church through suffering, and Christ would save her by His return at the end of the Tribulation when He would destroy Antichrist, deliver His Church, and bring the world to an end and inaugurate His millennial kingdom. The prevailing view is a posttribulation premillennialism.[18]

As observed earlier, Augustine's eschatological position became increasingly dominant during the Middle Ages and premillennialism went into virtual eclipse. Some segments of the Reformation were premillennial in orientation, and they were all of the posttribulational variety. Some of these sects experienced real opposition and even persecution—much of it religious in source and nature—so it is not surprising that these sects expected the church to remain on earth during the great tribulation. Not until pietism developed in the Lutheran church did premillennialism enter that body.[19] In the eighteenth and nineteenth centuries a large number of significant Bible scholars in Great Britain and America were premillennialists, among them Isaac Newton, Charles Wesley, Augustus Toplady, Richard C. Trench, Edward Bickersteth, Horatius Bonar, H. G. Guinness, C. J. Ellicott, Henry Alford, Joseph A. Seiss, and J. H. Raven. With the exception of the dispensationalist Plymouth Brethren, almost all were posttribulationists. Even among the Brethren there was diversity, Tregelles and Benjamin W. Newton advocating a form of posttribulationism.[20]

With the influence of dispensationalism spreading in conservative and fundamentalist circles, a virtual polarization occurred

---

17. *Treatise on Christ and Antichrist* 60–61.
18. *The Blessed Hope*, p. 31.
19. Clarence Beckwith, "Millennium," p. 376.
20. Ladd, *The Blessed Hope*, p. 41.

151

following World War I: one must be either amillennial or pretribulational. To be a premillennialist—a *real* premillennialist—was to be pretribulational as well, in the minds of many dispensationalists. Immediately following World War II, however, a movement arose popularly known as new evangelicalism, challenging many features of the dispensationalist-fundamentalist alliance. Although not the focus of their criticism, new evangelicals took issue with the doctrine of a pretribulational rapture. Such men as Edward J. Carnell and Ladd developed and expounded a posttribulational premillennialism.

Tenets of Posttribulationism

The Church's Presence in the Tribulation

The major contention of posttribulationism—within the context of this study—is that the church will be present in the tribulation. The church will be spared from the wrath of God but not from the tribulation.

The Greek word θυμός, meaning "a violent outburst of anger," is used of God's wrath nine of the eighteen times it appears in the New Testament. All nine of these are in the Book of Revelation, where the divine wrath is portrayed as striking only the wicked (in Rev. 14:8 it comes upon Babylon; in 14:19 and 19:15, the armies at Armageddon; in 15:1, 7 and 16:1, 19, the earth-dwellers). The Greek word ὀργή, meaning "a settled state of wrath," is used of God's anger about twenty-seven times in the New Testament. God's ὀργή, posttribulationists contend, falls only upon the wicked, never the righteous. The evidence supporting this contention is both positive and negative. Negatively, only the wicked are described as victims of this wrath (John 3:36; Rom. 1:18; II Thess. 1:8; Rev. 6:16–17; 14:10; 16:19; 19:15). Positively, it is stated that believers are: "saved by him [Christ] from the wrath of God" (Rom. 5:9), "delivered . . . from the wrath to come" (I Thess. 1:10 KJV), "not destined . . . for wrath" (I Thess. 5:9).[21]

In contrast with this, however, is the concept of tribulation, denoted by the noun θλῖψις and the verb θλίβω. Of the fifty-five

---

21. Gundry, *The Tribulation*, pp. 48–49; Ladd, *The Blessed Hope*, p. 122.

occurrences of these words in the New Testament, forty-seven relate to tribulation endured by saints. Only twice does the word refer to God's anger against sinners (Rom. 2:9; II Thess. 1:6), and in neither case is it God's anger against sinners during Daniel's seventieth week. In the context of the seventieth week, *tribulation* refers to the persecution of the saints (Matt. 24:9, 21, 29; Mark 13:19–24; Rev. 7:14). Tribulation, then, is not God's wrath against the sinners, but the wrath of Satan, Antichrist, and the wicked against the saints.[22]

The normal, typical experience of the saints is, according to numerous passages, that of tribulation. Jesus said, "In the world you have tribulation" (John 16:33). Paul and Barnabas preached that we must enter the kingdom of God through many tribulations (Acts 14:22). Paul even said, "We also exult in our tribulations" (Rom. 5:3 NASB). John identified himself to his readers as a "fellow-partaker in the tribulation . . . in Jesus" (Rev. 1:9 NASB). The church, destined to tribulations in general (I Thess. 3:3), has throughout this age been opposed and persecuted by many anti-christs (I John 2:18, 22; 4:3).[23]

Posttribulationists do not deny a distinction between tribulation in general and the great tribulation. They do note, however, that the word used to denote the general tribulation of the church is the same one used in Matthew 24:21 of the great tribulation. The difference between the latter and the former is one of degree, not of kind. It creates, therefore, a presumption that the church, having not been spared from persecution and trouble during any other period of time, will not be spared from that of the last times.[24]

These distinctions may seem insignificant, but they constitute a rejoinder to one argument of the pretribulationists, namely, that the church *must* be raptured from the world. John F. Walvoord put the argument thus: "Why should a child of God's grace—who is saved by grace, who is kept by grace, who has all the wonderful promises of God—be forced to go through a period which accord-

---

22. Gundry, *The Tribulation*, p. 49.
23. Ibid.
24. Ibid., p. 50.

ing to Scripture is expressly designed as a time of judgment upon a Christ-rejecting world?"[25] The posttribulationist agrees with the pretribulationist that the saints cannot and will not undergo the wrath of God. He argues, however, citing the foregoing linguistic data, that the church need not be raptured before the great tribulation.

But the Scripture does speak of a deliverance or a removal or an escape of the saints—presumably the church—from the trouble that awaits them. Does this not entail the idea of a rapture? A prime example is Jesus' exhortation to "watch at all times, praying that you may have strength to escape all these things that will take place, and to stand before the Son of man" (Luke 21:36). Posttribulationists such as Robert H. Gundry, however, have a way of handling this type of passage in a fashion consistent with their basic eschatological framework.

The context immediately preceding Luke 21:36, Gundry noted, indicates that Jesus' hearers would live in the time of the Antichrist and the tribulation. The pretribulationist frequently interprets this to mean that the disciples, being Jews, are representative of literal Israel, and hence that the elect who are present during the tribulation are elect Jews. To make this an evidence that the church will be raptured from the tribulation seems to be a rather strained interpretation. Further, the word translated "escape" is ἐκφεύγω, to "escape out of the midst of." Taking this word in its most obvious sense clearly contradicts the pretribulational tenet that the church will never find itself in the tribulation.[26]

A passage that has been the object of a great deal of scrutiny and controversy is Revelation 3:10: "Because you have kept my word of patient endurance, I will keep (τηρέω) you from (ἐκ) the hour of trial which is coming on the whole world, to try those who dwell upon the earth." The interpretation of this verse turns upon the significance of the preposition ἐκ. Posttribulationists argue basically that the primary sense of ἐκ, "emergence from within," refutes the pretribulational interpretation of the verse. For the church to emerge from within the hour of testing, it must have been present in that testing.[27]

25. *The Thessalonian Epistles,* p. 83.

26. Gundry, *The Tribulation,* p. 53.   27. Ibid., p. 55.

It is true that ἐκ and ἀπό ("away from") often denote the same relationship. In those cases, however, it is not because ἐκ has lost the idea of "out from within" but because ἀπό has added to its central meaning an additional one.[28]

John uses ἐκ approximately 336 times, far more often than any other New Testament writer. In every case the idea of emergence or origin is the meaning most suitable to the context. The Johannine usage of the word, then, appears to be well established.[29]

Pretribulationists sometimes object that if the posttribulational view is correct, then in place of ἐκ would be either διά ("through") or ἐν ("in"). Gundry replied that it is a matter of emphasis. Ἐν would have placed all the emphasis on presence within. Διά would have emphasized entrance, presence within, and emergency. But ἐκ puts all the emphasis upon emergence, thus highlighting the final, victorious outcome of the keeping and guarding. The same emphasis appears in Revelation 7:14, where the saints come "out of (ἐκ) the great tribulation." The important question, said Gundry, is why John did not use ἀπό in Revelation 3:10, which would at least *permit* a pretribulational interpretation, or why he did not use a preposition that would *require* this interpretation—ἐκτός, ἔξω, ἔξωθεν, ἄνευ, or χωρίς.[30]

The final issue in Revelation 3:10 is the meaning of the verb τηρέω. When a situation of danger is in view, τηρέω means to "guard." Danger is implicit in the idea of guarding. If the church is in heaven at this time, however, as pretribulationism teaches, then what can be the danger that requires God's protecting hand upon her? Throughout the Septuagint and the New Testament, τηρέω always denotes protection within the sphere of danger.[31]

In only one other place in the New Testament does τηρέω occur with ἐκ: "I do not pray that thou shouldst take (αἴρω) them out of (ἐκ) the world, but that thou shouldst keep (τηρέω) them from (ἐκ) the evil one" (John 17:15). Αἴρω ἐκ, which means "to lift, raise up, or remove," seems to describe perfectly what the

28. Ibid., p. 56.

29. Ibid., p. 57.

30. Ibid., pp. 57–58.

31. Ibid., p. 58.

rapture will be—a lifting up or removal. Yet it is in contrast and opposition to precisely this idea that Jesus uses τηρέω ἐκ in the second clause. It seems strange that in Revelation 3:10 τηρέω ἐκ can bear the very meaning it seems to oppose in John 17:15. Nor can the parallel between the two verses be eliminated by distinguishing a moral realm in John 17:15 and a physical realm in Revelation 3:10, for the physical presence of the disciples is what places them in the moral sphere of the evil one.[32]

The Meeting "in the Air"

Another major tenet of pretribulationism is its conception of believers meeting the Lord "in the air." When Christ comes *for* the saints before the tribulation, they will meet Him in the air and He will take them with Him to heaven for seven years. There they will await His triumphant return to set up His kingdom on earth. In the posttribulational frame of reference, however, the believers will be caught up to meet the Lord at the conclusion of the tribulation, and immediately they will accompany Him on His triumphant descent to the earth.

Which of these conceptions is supported by the meaning of ἀπάντησις, the word rendered "meet" in I Thessalonians 4:17? This is a crucial question. The posttribulationist argues that the meaning of ἀπάντησις fits his view better than it does the pretribulationist's.

This word appears in only two other places in the New Testament (the occurrence in Matthew 27:32 is textually suspect). An explicitly eschatological reference occurs in the parable of the wise and foolish virgins (Matt. 25:6). Here the cry of announcement when the bridegroom came was, "Behold, the bridegroom! Come out to meet (ἀπάντησις) him." How did the wise virgins respond? They went out as a welcoming party and met him somewhere outside the place where the marriage feast was to take place. They then turned around and accompanied or escorted him to the marriage feast. Presumably they did not interrupt the bridegroom's progress or reverse his direction; they and he did not depart to

---

32. Ibid., pp. 58–59.

some other place for an interlude after which they returned together.

The word also occurs in a narrative passage that is not eschatological, Acts 28:15–16. Here Paul and his party were approaching Rome. A group of brethren in Rome, when they heard of the
group's approach, went out as far as the Forum of Appius and
Three Taverns "to meet" (ἀπάντησις) them. This was very encour-
aging to Paul, and he and the welcoming party continued on
together to Rome. Here again, the term is used of a welcoming
party that comes out to meet a guest and then returns with him to
his destination.

If this is the basic meaning of ἀπάντησις, how then can we
interpret I Thessalonians 4:17? Christ will return, and the righteous
dead will be resurrected to meet Him, followed by the believers
who are yet alive upon the earth. These two groups will become
one great welcoming party, and when they meet the Lord, He will
not turn around and withdraw with them. Rather they will turn
around and accompany Him to earth. The word ἀπάντησις has
exactly the same meaning here that it has in the other two New
Testament references, particularly in Matthew 25:6. Nothing in the
comparative study of the word suggests a withdrawal of believers
to some other place, as the pretribulational view seems to
require.[33]

The Restrainer's Removal

One other significant passage is II Thessalonians 2:6–7: "And
you know what is restraining him now so that he may be revealed
in his time. For the mystery of lawlessness is already at work; only
he who now restrains it will do so until he is out of the way." The
standard pretribulational interpretation of the restrainer identifies
him with the Holy Spirit. Since the Holy Spirit now resides within
the church, to take him out of the way necessarily requires the
rapture or removal of the church from the world.

Posttribulationists interpret this passage in one of two basic
ways: (1) the restrainer is the Holy Spirit, but His withdrawal does
not entail the removal of the church; or (2) the restrainer is not the

---

33. Ladd, *The Blessed Hope,* pp. 90–92.

Holy Spirit. Both interpretations agree, however, that the removal of that which restrains is not the rapture of the church.

Ladd is representative of those who do not identify the restrainer with the Holy Spirit. He feels that the expression "until he is out of the way" (literally, "until he comes out of the midst") may not refer to the restraining power at all but to the Antichrist. The restraining power then would be the power of God Himself and the passage would be paraphrased: "For the mystery of lawlessness already is working; only there is one who restrains now, namely God, until he, the Antichrist, arises out of the midst." Ladd asserted that this rendering best fits the organization of verses 6 and 7. These two verses say precisely the same thing, and there is a similar balance in the two parts of each verse.

> 6a And now ye know that which restraineth [the power of God],
> 6b to the end that he [Antichrist] may be revealed in his own season.
> For the mystery of lawlessness doth already work:
> 7a only there is one [God] that restraineth now
> 7b until he [Antichrist] be taken out of the way. (ASV)

Ladd readily admitted that this is an unauthoritative interpretation, but he claimed that it is at least as possible as the one which makes the restrainer the Holy Spirit, and that it "fits the movement of the passage more naturally." In any event he said that any claim to find in this passage support for a pretribulation rapture is nothing more than an assumption.[34]

Gundry has enunciated the other posttribulational interpretation of the restrainer, namely, that the restrainer is the Holy Spirit. His first reason is that this view was held by some in the early church. Second, it would seem that to restrain a person, another person is necessary. Third, this interpretation best explains the change from neuter ("that which restraineth," τὸ κατέχον) to masculine gender ("one that restraineth," ὁ κατέχων): Paul first referred to the restrainer as neuter because the word Πνεῦμα ("Spirit") is neuter, and then referred to the restrainer as masculine because the Spirit has personality.[35]

---

34. Ibid., p. 95.
35. *The Tribulation,* p. 125.

The pretribulational interpretation of the restrainer, say post-tribulationists, has some real difficulties. For one thing, Jesus clearly implied that the Holy Spirit will be present during the tribulation. He said to those who would be His witnesses during that period, ". . . it is not you who speak, but the Holy Spirit" (Mark 13:11). During the tribulation the Spirit will apparently empower believers for evangelism and will regenerate on an even greater scale than He does now. Despite the increase in Satanic activity, the results of the Holy Spirit's working will be more evident then than now. This should require an increase in, not a diminution of, the Spirit's work. Nor is it correct to think of the Spirit as never operating apart from the church. It is quite possible that the Spirit can restrain the evil one without using the church, and then can withhold that restraining power without removing the church or indeed even without stopping His work in general.[36]

Evaluation of Posttribulationism

Positive Aspects

One of posttribulationism's greatest strengths is its versatility in dealing with Scripture. This scheme of interpretation seems to take into account the broadest sweep of Scripture. It offers suitable and plausible interpretations of all types of relevant Biblical material—the apocalyptic writings, the prophetic books, the eschatological teachings of Jesus, and much more. In other words, it is not based upon a few carefully selected proof texts.

Not only does it draw upon a wide swath of Scripture, but it seems to handle those Scriptures more naturally than does pretribulationism. By and large, posttribulational interpretations of key passages appear to fit well the natural sense of those passages. That is, posttribulationism does not depend upon unearthing secret meanings. For example, when the Scripture speaks of tribulation saints, elect, and the like, posttribulationism does not give a meaning to them that is radically different from their meaning elsewhere in the Bible. They are simply the same kind of believers that are referred to from the time of Christ onward. Similarly, the removal of the church is not somehow "smuggled" into texts (such as

---

36. Ibid., pp. 126–28.

II Thess. 2:3) that on the surface refer to apostasy. While the term ἀποστασία may surely mean a departure in some sense other than the most common or frequent sense, the most common or natural meaning should be assumed unless the context requires a specialized meaning. In the absence of such contextual indications, the normal meaning ought to obtain. In this respect posttribulationism seems to handle Scripture more smoothly and adequately than does pretribulationism.

Another way of putting this is that posttribulationism displays less of a tendency than its competitor to read preconceived ideas into a text. It seldom finds in a text special ideas that one would find only if he came to the text with a preconceived system. On the other hand, its interpretations of passages, while natural, do not conflict with posttribulational conceptions.

Posttribulationism also counters well what has been referred to colloquially as the cop-out mentality. After 1918 American fundamentalism showed strong otherworldly tendencies, causing many adherents to neglect present responsibilities while dwelling upon the hope of a heavenly home. In eschatology this finds expression in the wish that the church will be "raptured" out of the world so that it need not undergo the great tribulation. Posttribulationism offers no escape from hardship. It paints a very realistic picture of the demands and costs and pain of the Christian life, while reminding believers of the resources of power upon which they can draw when living in the midst of hardship.

Finally, posttribulationism offers a basis for Christian anticipation. It does not claim to have worked out all the details of the last things or to have explained fully all the symbols involved in Biblical eschatology, and it has generally exercised real restraint and care in setting dates. In so doing, it has managed to preserve something of the genuine sense of mystery about the Biblical revelation. There is both a confidence in the major facts of eschatology and a belief that when the Lord comes, the remaining facts will be revealed and the reception of this revelation will constitute part of the joy of the consummation of God's plan.

Negative Aspects

There are, however, certain negative features in posttribulationism as it is generally formulated. One is the relative vagueness of much of it. Whereas pretribulationists speak of the millennium as precisely one thousand years and the tribulation as exactly seven years, the posttribulationist frequently is unsure of the length of each. He simply knows that there will be such periods. This makes the millennium rather colorless. The relative lack of concrete detail concerning the millennium results in relatively little rationale for a millennium. Similarly the relative absence of unequivocal meanings for eschatological symbols in Scripture gives to posttribulationism less rhetorical persuasiveness than pretribulationism generally has. In some respects and on some issues, posttribulationism is virtually indistinguishable from amillennialism.

There is also often a lack of positive affirmation on the part of posttribulationism. In part this is due to its having in recent years been largely enunciated in reaction and contrast to pretribulationism, and therefore being identified as the view that the church will *not* be raptured prior to the great tribulation. In part, this results from the fact that its major doctrine is an unpleasant one, namely, believers will have to undergo severe tribulation.

Further, however, many posttribulationists simply have not been eager to enunciate their position. In those environments in which pretribulationism has at times been virtually tantamount to orthodoxy, some posttribulationist pastors have refused to be dogmatic about their position and thus have appeared to lack conviction or even understanding.

Because posttribulationism considers fine nuances of meaning and precise definitions in eschatology to be less important than does pretribulationism, it has not stressed the intensive study of eschatology that pretribulationism has. In the desire to avoid hairsplitting, it has at times overreacted and hence failed to emphasize sufficiently the great central eschatological facts, such as the glorious, bodily, second coming of the Lord. In a time of broad, resurgent interest in eschatology, this must surely be considered a demerit.

Chapter 9

Mediating Positions

In the two immediately preceding chapters we have discussed two views that are not only contradictory but also contrary. They are diametrically opposite on essential points.

Because each position is supported by considerations possessing some degree of cogency and because these two views are contraries, we should expect some mediating positions also to arise, positions that incorporate salient features of both pretribulationism and posttribulationism. Such views have indeed been put forth, and we will discuss three of them in this chapter: the midtribulational view, the partial rapture view, and the imminent posttribulational view. A very brief statement of each of these will help orient us for the more complete statement of each that will follow.

Midtribulationism teaches that the church will be present on earth during, and thus will experience, a portion of the tribulation, but then will be removed before the worst of the tribulation. The partial-rapture view sees one segment of the church being raptured before the tribulation and another segment remaining on earth through the entire tribulation. Thus the rapture is pretribulational for some believers and posttribulational for others. The final position understands Christ's coming as being both imminent and post-tribulational. These three views may therefore be differentiated in terms of what they split: (1) the duration of the tribulation, (2) the body of believers, and (3) the bond between the imminent and the pretribulational coming of Christ.

Midtribulational View

Midtribulationism is the view that the church will go through the first half of what is identified as the great tribulation, or the seven years of Daniel's seventieth week of years. While somewhat oversimplified, this statement represents the position fairly accurately. Two leading recent exponents of this position are James O. Buswell, Jr., (1895–1976) and Norman B. Harrison (1874–1960).

A first salient feature of this theory is that the "elect" spoken of by Jesus in the great eschatological discourse (e.g., Matt. 24:22; Mark 13:20) are not Jews; they are saints in the usual sense of the church. Buswell argued for this on two grounds:[1]

1. The Gospels of Matthew and Mark were written some time after Paul's epistles had been written and circulated. Paul's vocabulary and the meaning he gave to words would thus have been familiar to believers of that day. It is reasonable to expect that if the Lord had meant by "the elect" something different from what Paul had meant by the expression in such passages as Romans 8:33, then Matthew and Mark would have given some indication of that, thereby avoiding confusion. But no indication of this is present in the Gospels.

2. It is apparent that Christ, here answering questions put to Him by the apostles, was speaking not to them only, but to the entire church throughout the present age. He was in the habit of coupling together references to the apostles and the entire church, as in the great commission (Matt. 28:18–20), the high-priestly prayer of John 17 (especially v. 20), and many other priceless portions of our Christian heritage. In particular, when Jesus in Matthew 24:15ff. told of the destruction of Jerusalem, He spoke first in the third person ("when *you* see . . .") and then in the third person. He referred to the Jews as "they," not "you," considering them a separate people who would suffer at that time and throughout the age.

Further, Jesus' warning regarding the abomination of desolation (Matt. 24:15) seemed to Buswell definitely parallel to Paul's warn-

---

1. *A Systematic Theology of the Christian Religion,* 2:393–94.

ing to the Thessalonians (II Thess. 2:4). But the Thessalonian believers were not primarily Jewish but Gentile![2]

Nor was Buswell impressed by the argument that Jesus must
have been referring to Israel because the fig tree in the parable
(Matt. 24:32–35) is a "type" of Israel. There is, he said, no sufficient ground for limiting the fig tree to Israel. Indeed, this parable
is introduced in Luke with the words "Look at the fig tree, *and all
the trees*" (21:29), proving that on this occasion Jesus did not have
this narrow application in mind.[3] It is apparent that Buswell did
not share one of the distinctive conceptions of the pretribulationists, and particularly of dispensationalists, namely, that "the elect"
of the Olivet discourse are Jews rather than the church.

A second major tenet of this view is a distinction between tribulation and wrath. In this respect midtribulationism resembles posttribulationism, which sees the church as present during both the
tribulation and the wrath of God, but shielded from the latter.
Midtribulationism relates these two sequentially. The church is
present during the tribulation but is removed prior to the outpouring of God's wrath.

The tribulation is to be very severe but very brief. Jesus in-
structed His disciples to watch carefully for the appearance in the
temple's holy place of the "abomination of desolation," an event
of which Daniel had spoken. As reported by both Matthew and
Mark, Jesus then indicated both the severity and the brevity of the
tribulation: "For then there will be great tribulation, such as has
not been from the beginning of the world until now, no, and never
will be. And if those days had not been shortened, no human being
would be saved; but for the sake of the elect those days will be
shortened." (Matt. 24:21–22; cf. Mark 13:19–20)[4]

As terrible as this tribulation will be, however, it should not be
identified with the time of the wrath of God. The Lord, after
describing the tribulation, enumerated signs that will follow it.
Great cosmic upheavals will occur "immediately after the tribulation of those days" (Matt. 24:29; cf. Mark 13:24–25; Luke
21:25–26). Buswell took the reference to these portents coming

---

2. Ibid., pp. 391, 394.

3. Ibid., p. 394.

4. Ibid., p. 388.

"after the tribulation of those days" to mean that the vials of God's wrath will be poured out, not during "the great tribulation," but subsequent to it. Tribulation is not unique to the last times. It is the common lot of the church in every age. Although this tribulation will be uniquely severe, it will not, according to Buswell's characterization of it, be qualitatively without parallel. Since tribulation generally speaking is man's wrath against God's people, tribulation is the lot of the church in all ages.[5]

The wrath of God, however, is not for the church. Several references indicate that salvation is deliverance *from* the wrath of God. "We shall be saved from wrath through him" (Rom. 5:9 KJV). The church is "to wait for his [God's] Son from heaven, whom he raised from the dead, Jesus who delivers us from the wrath to come" (I Thess. 1:10; cf. Matt. 3:7; Luke 3:7). "God has not destined us for wrath, but to obtain salvation through our Lord Jesus Christ" (I Thess. 5:9). Buswell summarized by saying, "Although these references to salvation from wrath do not definitely state, in themselves, that the rapture of the church will take place before the outpouring of the vials of wrath, yet these references harmonize with that view."[6]

There are, however, more specific proofs that the church will be raptured before the vials of wrath are poured out. Certain details come to the midpoint of this seven-year period (the tribulation). The "abomination" comes "in the midst of the seven," that is, the middle of the seven-year period. This abomination is identified with the "coming," the parousia, of the man of sin (II Thess. 2:9), which is also when he will be revealed (II Thess. 2:3). This in turn is identical with the coming to power of the little horn (Dan. 7:24–25), who is permitted to continue for 3½ years (Dan. 7:25b). All of these details taken collectively illustrate how well the midtribulational view fits the whole of Scriptural data and accounts for it.[7]

In terms of locating the rapture within the occurrences mentioned in the Book of Revelation, midtribulationists place it at the

---

5. Ibid., p. 389.

6. Ibid.

7. Ibid., pp. 390–93, 457.

sounding of the seventh trumpet (Rev. 11:15).[8] The time of wrath for the unrighteous and the time of rewards for the righteous dead begin simultaneously. The seventh trumpet announces both the wrath of God and rewards for the righteous dead.

> "... the nations raged, but thy wrath came,
>   and the time for the dead to be judged,
> for rewarding thy servants, the prophets and saints,
>   and those who fear thy name, both small and great,
> and for destroying the destroyers of the earth."
>   (Rev. 11:18)

Harrison also placed the coming of Christ and the rapture at this point. Up until verse 17 Christ is ordinarily referred to in Revelation as the one "who is and who was and who is to come." But in verse 17 the future tense is omitted for the first time: "We give thanks to thee, Lord God Almighty, who art and who wast...." (v. 17). Harrison commented: "It seeks to tell us: He has come!"[9] He sees other evidences, also, in the reference to the cloud in 11:12. The cloud symbolized the Lord's presence many times in Israel's history: when He led them out of Egypt and through the wilderness, when He spoke with Moses, and when He filled the tabernacle and later the temple with His glory. So also it was the visible evidence of Christ's presence when He ascended to heaven, and so it will be when He returns (Acts 1:9; Luke 21:27).

There is in this view one very strong point of resemblance to classical pretribulationism: the separation of the second coming into two stages or phases. "Christ will return," Buswell wrote, "not only *for* His saints (John 14:3; I Thess. 4:16–18) but also He will come *with* His saints (Jude 14–15; Revelation 19:11–16)."[10]

Buswell and Harrison do differ somewhat in their terminology. Buswell spoke of the first half of the seven-year period, the half in which the church will be present, as the *tribulation,* and of the second half, from which the church will be absent, as the *wrath* of God.[11] Harrison, on the other hand, pointed out that John found

---

8. Ibid., pp. 396–98, 450ff.

9. *The End: Re-Thinking the Revelation,* p. 118.

10. *Systematic Theology,* 2:483.

11. Ibid., p. 389.

the first half of the seven years "sweet," the second half "bitter" (Rev. 10:9). The second half, then, is the "great tribulation." "This should suffice," Harrison wrote, "to correct the inexcusable confusing of the 7-year period and the Tribulation period, as though the two were synonymous and synchronous."[12] Harrison identified the tribulation with God's wrath: "Let us get clearly in mind the nature of the Tribulation, that it is divine 'wrath' (11:18; 14:8, 10, 19; 15:1, 7; 16:1, 19) and divine 'judgment' (14:7; 15:4; 16:7; 17:1; 18:10; 19:2)."[13]

Whatever terminology is employed, the idea is the same: the church is present during the first half of the period, undergoing persecution or troubles that are relatively light. The church is then raptured before the wrath of God, which is very severe, is poured out. The coming of Christ *with* the saints occurs at the end of this period. These ideas are sometimes blended in the popular expression: "Posttrib; pre–great trib."

We should note that advocates of this position do not use the expression *midtribulationism* to describe it. This is simply a designation given this position by nonadherents. It seems that on their own definitions, Buswell would term himself a posttribulationist and Harrison a pretribulationist.

We conclude with an evaluation of this approach, which has attempted to interpret realistically the term *elect* in Christ's great eschatological discourse. Its interpretation appears to be more natural than that of the pretribulationist. Buswell's argument seems basically sound.

On the other hand, the argument that the church is removed prior to the outpouring of God's wrath is quite inferential. Even if one establishes that believers cannot and should not undergo divine wrath, it does not necessarily follow that the church cannot be physically present. During the plagues of Egypt, the Israelites were in Egypt but the plagues were applied selectively. They came upon the Egyptians but not the Israelites. So it may well be with God's great wrath. The burden of proof still rests upon the midtribulationists to show that the church is removed before God pours out His wrath.

---

12. *The End,* p. 111.
13. Ibid., p. 120.

Partial-Rapture View

According to the partial-rapture view not all believers are raptured at one time, either before the great tribulation or after. Rather, believers are raptured in groups, as they are ready. This view is not widely held or known. In modern times it was first propounded by Robert G. Govett (1813–1901) as early as 1852. In the twentieth century it has been very capably stated and defended by George H. Lang. *The Dawn* magazine, published in London, also supported this view.

One key theological issue involved in this view, recognized by both its adherents and its opponents, is that translation is based upon reward. Ira E. David stated the partial-rapture view this way:

> The basis of translation must be grace or reward. Those who expect all in the real Church to be translated at once, think of translation as wholly of grace. Salvation is of grace. "By grace are ye saved through faith; and that not of yourselves: it is the gift of God." But after people are saved, they are rewarded for faithfulness and watchfulness. Repeatedly believers are warned against lack of these. In I Corinthians 3:14, 15, we are told of rewards for believers. "He shall receive a reward." Now is translation a reward? We believe that frequent exhortations in the Scriptures to watch, to be faithful, to be ready for Christ's coming, to live Spirit-filled lives, all suggest that translation is a reward.[14]

Advocates of this position feel that it sheds light upon a number of Scripture passages, particularly the eschatological parables. These distinguish between those taken and those left, those rewarded and those not rewarded. An instructive example of this is the parable of the wise and foolish virgins.

The popular interpretation suggests that the five wise virgins were genuine believers, the five foolish virgins hypocrites. Those who advocate the partial-rapture theory, by contrast, maintain that all ten were genuine believers. The distinction, then, is not between genuine and ungenuine believers, but between faithful and unfaithful ones. Govett advanced eight reasons for this interpretation: (1) All ten women are virgins, not merely pretenders to virginity. *They* do not call themselves virgins; *the Lord* does. (2) All ten have

---

14. "Translation: When Does It Occur?," pp. 358–59.

lighted torches, meaning that their professions of faith are supported by good works. (3) They go forth with a desire to meet Jesus, an indication of a truly converted heart. (4) Their torches burn some hours, an indication that they have the oil of grace. The text is not explicit about whether or not their torches ever do go out. (5) They are accounted worthy to attain the first resurrection, the resurrection from among the dead, which is true only of the children of God. (6) The foolish virgins sleep with the wise and awake with them. (7) The foolish virgins are ready to enter in if the bridegroom comes early rather than late, that is, before they fall asleep. (8) Even at the last they are virgins, the essential *internal* qualification for the wedding supper. Their only deficiency is in the realm of *circumstantial* and *secondary* fitness—they lack a second measure of oil. Unbelievers, by contrast, fail to meet both qualifications.[15]

Govett concluded that the parable teaches that just before the Savior appears, those who have neglected to apply for the gifts of the Holy Spirit will be excluded from a peculiar occasion of festivity and joy—the wedding supper. This parable, however, does not speak of the church of Christ as a whole—only of "believers *who have fallen asleep, or who shall fall asleep, ere Jesus appears.*"[16]

Another passage appealed to by advocates of the partial-rapture view is Matthew 24:40: "Then two men will be in the field; one is taken (παραλαμβάνω) and one is left." This can be understood in one of two ways: (1) this is a taking unto wrath, in which case being taken is a dishonor and being left is an honor; or (2) this is a taking unto mercy, in which case the significances are reversed. It is not, however, a taking unto wrath, for the word used for "taking" is quite different from the one used to describe the destruction wrought by the deluge: ". . . the flood came, and *took* (αἴρω) them all away" (v. 39 KJV). Παραλαμβάνω, which is used by Luke as well as Matthew in this discourse, conveys the idea of taking someone as a companion by one's side. It is used, for example, of the evil spirit's choice of companions (Matt. 12:45).

Govett also noted that Jesus attached a warning or caution against spiritual burdens. This is appropriate if the hearers were

---

15. *The Saints' Rapture to the Presence of the Lord Jesus*, pp. 126–28.
16. Ibid., p. 129.

believers, but not if they were both believers and unbelievers. Govett summarized Jesus' teaching: " 'Take heed to *yourselves,'* as regards your *moral state,* is the cry to the church; 'beware of things *without,'* is the call to the *earthly elect."*[17] Govett concluded, then, that this parable refers to the rapture; both are believers, the one taken being a watchful believer, the one left being unwatchful.

> I conclude, then, that nothing but the rapture will satisfy the conditions of the parable, and that the two are believers. To unbelievers it would be neither loss nor shame to be left. The two are suited companions of each other, but not equally ready to be companions of Messiah. Friend is severed from friend, and the loss is both more startling than that of the stranger, and answers so nearly to the separation between the wicked and the just, as to be deeply painful to the one left behind.[18]

One other passage used to support this view is Luke 21:36: "Watch ye therefore, and pray always, that ye may be accounted worthy to escape all these things that shall come to pass, and to stand before the Son of man" (KJV).

Lang saw five distinct declarations in this text: (1) Escape is possible from all those things of which Christ had been speaking, that is, from the whole of the end times. (2) The day of testing will be universal and unavoidable by any then on earth. Any who are to escape it must be removed from the earth. (3) Those who are to escape will be taken to where the Son of man is at that time, that is, at the throne of the Father in the heavens. They will stand before Him there. (4) There is a fearful peril of disciples becoming worldly in heart and thus being enmeshed in that last period. (5) Hence it is needful to watch and pray ceaselessly, so that we may prevail over all obstacles and dangers and thus escape that era.[19]

Lang saw this as very definite and clear evidence for the partial-rapture view. He stated that this text sets aside the opinion that all Christians will escape, irrespective of their moral state. "There is a door of escape: but as with all doors, only those who are awake

---

17. "One Taken and One Left," p. 518.
18. Ibid.
19. *The Revelation of Jesus Christ: Select Studies,* pp. 88–89.

will see it, and only those who are in earnest will reach it before the storm bursts."[20]

We may note, then, three salient features of the partial-rapture theory: (1) Translation is a reward for faithfulness and watchfulness. It is not wholly of grace. (2) Not all believers will be raptured at the same time. Those who are faithful and watchful will be taken before the others. (3) There will also be a partial resurrection of believers, on much the same basis as the partial rapture.

Now we must evaluate this somewhat novel theory. On the positive side, we must grant that this is something of a breakthrough in attempting to do justice to two sets of data that are seemingly in conflict. It allows both for the imminence of the Lord's second coming and for the presence of the church (believers) in the tribulation. It also offers a creative exegesis of some relevant passages, finding possible meanings that might otherwise be overlooked.

One negative criticism, made particularly by conventional pretribulationists, is that the partial-rapture view is based on a principle of works, which is in opposition to the Scriptural teaching on grace. These critics see the translation and resurrection of the church as part of the salvation provided for it by grace. John F. Walvoord commented:

> To accept a works principle for this important aspect of salvation is to undermine the whole concept of justification by faith through grace, the presence of the Holy Spirit as the seal of God "unto the day of redemption" (Eph. 4:30), and the entire tremendous undertaking of God on behalf of those who trust Him. The issue of reward is properly settled at the judgment seat of Christ, not before, and not in a partial translation resulting in the infliction of the tribulation on other believers.[21]

But this criticism misses the mark. Walvoord himself admitted that there will be rewards and presumably (in the absence of any denial of this specific point) he believes they will be based on works. If this is the case, then the issue between Walvoord and advocates of the partial rapture is not really that of salvation by grace or by

---

20. Ibid., p. 89.
21. *The Rapture Question,* pp. 124–25.

works. Rather the issue is either (1) when the reward will be given, or (2) whether the rapture is part of the process of salvation or one of the rewards. These points are the proper focus of debate.

Further, there is a way of stating the partial-rapture view that avoids this criticism. It can be maintained that inclusion in (preliminary stages of) the rapture is indeed a reward for faithfulness and watchfulness, but that such faithfulness and watchfulness are accomplished by the grace of God; they are not human accomplishments, as works are often thought to be. Though Govett did not state his belief in this way, he could have, the point being that the problem of "salvation by works" is not inherent in the partial-rapture theory.

A more telling difficulty with this view is the exegesis underlying it. Too much is read into the passages. For example, the suggestion that the one taken and the one left are both believers rests upon the assumption that Christ's injunction could have meaning only for believers. This is a rather gratuitous assumption, however. Here, as with the parable of the virgins, the preparedness being urged may well include the acceptance of salvation or a decision for Christ. If the meaning attached to these parables by advocates of the partial-rapture view were really intended, it would be more clearly and explicitly stated.

Imminent Posttribulational View

The major proponent of imminent posttribulationism, J. Barton Payne, argues in his book *The Imminent Appearing of Christ* that the appearing of Christ is imminent, but that it will follow, not precede, the great tribulation. Payne chose the title of his book intentionally and carefully. Pretribulationists have customarily distinguished the coming of Christ (His coming *for* the church) from the appearing of Christ (His coming *with* the church). They hold the former to be pretribulational and imminent, the latter to be posttribulational and not imminent. Conventional posttribulationists, on the other hand, hold to a unified return of Christ (including both His coming and His appearing) which will be posttribulational and therefore is not imminent. By speaking of the *imminent appearing,* Payne clearly distinguished his view from both pre- and posttribulationism.

Although not the first point in Payne's presentation, the most convenient one with which to begin is that of imminency. The word *imminent* conveys the idea of something impending, hanging over, about to overtake one. It means, in this case, that the coming of Christ could be so swift as to give no real forewarning or opportunity to make preparations. Payne was careful to indicate that this does not mean that Christ's coming *must* be soon, only that it *may* be soon. This, then, is the issue: Can the coming of Christ be soon, or must some events inevitably intervene?[22]

Two classes of New Testament words characterize the believer's attitude toward the second coming of Christ: verbs of watching and verbs of waiting. The two primary verbs of the first class are γρηγορέω ("to be awake") and ἀγρυπνέω ("to be sleepless"). Both involve immediate vigilance. While they are suitable for expressing the hope of Christ's imminent appearing, they do not *require* that His appearing be imminent.[23] In an advent context the injunction to watch may mean simply to watch oneself, that is, one's own immediate spiritual state. It may, however, mean to watch for an event, in which case watching is displayed by preparedness. If the event for which one is to watch can in some way be dated, like the flood in Noah's time, imminence is not involved. If, however, the time of the coming event is unknown, then the command to watch for it does mean that the event is imminent.

The verbs of waiting are primarily δέχομαι ("receive, endure") and its compounds, ἐκδέχομαι ("expect, wait") and προσδέχομαι ("welcome, wait for"); and μένω (which means "remain" but which in its transitive usage means "wait") and its compound, περιμένω ("welcome, wait for"). The idea of waiting, when undefined, suggests imminence, but these words are sometimes also used of happenings that are specifically said not to be imminent.[24] Scripture sometimes even enjoins waiting for or exercising patience with respect to Christ's coming, but without using any of these verbs; accompanying statements, though, suggest that His return is near at hand. All depends upon the context.

---

22. *The Imminent Appearing of Jesus Christ,* pp. 85–86.
23. Ibid., pp. 86–87.
24. Ibid., p. 87.

It is often objected, however, that when the passages that urge the readers to watch and wait were written, they could not have required their early readers to believe in imminence. Certain events had to be fulfilled before Christ would come. But if these passages did not require their early readers to believe in the imminence of Christ's coming, they do not require us to believe it either.

There are a large number of such events.[25] The Holy Spirit, the Comforter, was to come and replace Jesus among the disciples (John 16:7). Pentecost, to be sure, was only about ten days removed, but Jesus' prediction that the Spirit would guide the disciples into all the truth (v. 13) and bring to remembrance all that He had said to them (14:26) suggests a considerably longer period of elapsed time. Christ had commissioned the apostles to make disciples of all nations and had promised to be with them always, "even unto the end of the world" (Matt. 28:20 KJV). They were to be witnesses unto the uttermost part of the earth (Acts 1:8), which assumed that the gospel would be preached "in the whole world" (Matt. 26:13).

Paul, at his call to be an apostle, was told what would be the general course of his life (Acts 9:15), including his testimony before kings (cf. 22:15; 26:2) and his reaching Rome and Caesar (23:11; 27:24; cf. 28:30). Paul gave an inspired prediction of his own death (II Tim. 4:5ff.), and Peter was told by the Lord that he would experience death before the second advent took place (John 21:18ff.).

Finally, Christ had predicted certain specific historical events preceding the last days (Luke 21:9): specifically, Jerusalem would fall (A.D. 70) and "the times of the Gentiles" would be fulfilled (v. 24). Paul also stated about A.D. 50 that the day of the Lord could not come (II Thess. 2:2) until the Antichrist and a major apostasy had come (v. 3).

In light of all of these considerations, Payne conceded that the early apostolic church could not have expected the Lord to come at any moment.[26] Nonetheless, in reply to the disciples' question, "Will you at this time restore the kingdom to Israel?", Jesus did not simply give a flat no. He parried the question by saying, "It is

---

25. Ibid., pp. 88–90.

26. Ibid., p. 90.

not for you to know. . . ." (Acts 1:7). Even in those days, the end could have come within the lifetime of those addressed. Payne pointed out that all of the predictions that postponed the hope of the first Christians "a few years" were adequately fulfilled within a period of fifty years. The gospel had been taken into all of the ancient world, Christians had been persecuted, Peter and Paul had been martyred. Thus, no unfulfilled prediction any longer prevented the return of Jesus Christ from taking place at any time. Payne further countered criticism in this way:

> That a position of qualified imminency has therefore been possible for the church is not to be denied. But that the church today ought to be characterized by a similar, "soon but not today" expectation would seemingly have to be grounded on the assumption that we now stand where the early church did, namely, with the same, more than momentary, unfulfilled antecedents to Christ's return. . . . such is no longer the case. [27]

Although John and Peter knew that some events must intervene, that did not prevent them from teaching and practicing a hope in imminence. Christ also knew that Jerusalem would have to fall before His return, but He still taught his disciples that after its destruction they should look for His coming as near (Luke 21:24–27). To summarize Payne's view: at the time of their writing, the injunctions regarding watching and waiting could not have entailed a strict imminency for the immediate recipients, since certain events must occur before the Lord could return. Because those events have now transpired, however, nothing prevents those injunctions from teaching imminence. Instead of deciding in advance what the Scripture writers could have said, we should exegete what they did say. [28]

Payne observed that a number of references to watching and waiting for the Lord are not relevant to the discussion of imminency. Among these are I Thessalonians 5:6, II Thessalonians 3:5 (KJV), Hebrews 9:28, I Peter 4:7 (KJV), and Revelation 3:3. Either these passages refer to the believer watching and keeping himself, or they refer to watching for the Lord in such a general

---

27. Ibid., n. 12.
28. Ibid., p. 91.

way that it applies to His work as a whole rather than specifically to the second coming.[29]

Several passages, however, do support imminence. Among these are Matthew 24:42–25:13 (cf. Mark 13:33–37 and Luke 21:34–36); Luke 12:36–40; Romans 8:19, 23, 25; I Corinthians 1:7; Philippians 3:20; 4:5; I Thessalonians 1:9–10; Titus 2:12–13; James 5:7–8; Jude 21; and Revelation 16:15. Each stresses one or more of the following factors: the importance of watchfulness; the uncertainty of the time of coming; and, as a necessary corollary of the latter, the possibility that He could come now, although it is certainly not the case that He *must*.[30]

The other part of Payne's view is that the church's hope is for a deliverance from the world subsequent to the tribulation rather than for a rapture prior to the great tribulation. Payne argued that ten passages determine the relative time of the church's hope.

One of the most crucial passages is Matthew 24:29–31 (as well as the parallels, Mark 13:24–27 and Luke 21:25–27): "Immediately after the tribulation of those days . . . he will send out his angels with a loud trumpet call, and they will gather his elect from the four winds, from one end of heaven to the other." This certainly sounds like a rapture of the church following the tribulation.

Some pretribulationists, however, have replied that it refers not to the church but to elect Jews who have been converted during the tribulation.[31] Payne found this indefensible. The audience here is the disciples, to whom Jesus two evenings later promised Pentecost (John 14:16) and said: "Take, eat; this is my body" (Matt. 26:26). If the disciples represented the church on Thursday (Matt. 26), they represented the church on Tuesday (Matt. 24). Jesus ordinarily used the term *elect* of any whom he had chosen, but this discourse of Jesus was a private one for His disciples (Matt. 24:3) after He had publicly ended His ministry to Israel (23:38). Earlier that same day he had equated the word *elect* with those who were faithful to Him (22:14), with any nation, in fact, *except* Israel (21:43).[32]

---

29. Ibid., pp. 93–95.
30. Ibid., pp. 95–103.
31. Ibid., p. 55.
32. Ibid.

Other pretribulationists escape the apparent posttribulational teaching of this passage by saying that the sequence of predicted events is not strictly chronological. According to this argument, Matthew 24:32–25:30, with its exhortation to watchfulness for Christ's parousia, refers to Christ's coming for the church prior to the tribulation. The preceding section, however, which describes the gathering of the elect after the Lord's appearing (24:31), refers to His establishment of His kingdom after the tribulation. To account for this awkward chronology, pretribulationists suggest that through verse 31 Christ was accommodating Himself to the earthly (Jewish) orientation with which the disciples were saturated.[33] Payne found this interpretation as artificial and inadequate as the previous one. Without any apparent transition, Christ (according to this view) suddenly stopped speaking to the disciples as Jews and started addressing them as leaders of the church. He then warned them of an event (His coming for the church) that he had not previously mentioned and of which they had no knowledge. Further, in verses 37 and 39 He used the same word, *parousia,* of this hope of the church that he had just used of His "later" appearance to set up the earthly (Jewish) kingdom, and the same word that had been used in the original question (v. 3). Either Jesus allowed the disciples to confuse the two separate events (as some defenders of pretribulationism maintain) or Jesus Himself did not distinguish between these two events. The former alternative seems inconsistent with Jesus' other actions and teachings. Only the latter is a viable possibility.[34]

Space will not permit us to examine Payne's treatment of other passages: Luke 17:24; Romans 8:18–21; I Corinthians 15:51–52; II Thessalonians 1:6–8; 2:1–2; Titus 2:12–13; Revelation 7:3–4; 14:3–4; 20:4–5. Matthew 24:29–31 is perhaps the most crucial passage, and Payne's approach to it is representative of his approach to these other texts. He also considered several "contributory passages,"[35] which are less pointed in their thrust, and noted a number of "irrelevant passages."[36]

---

33. Ibid., p. 56.

34. Ibid., pp. 56–57.

35. Ibid., pp. 65–71.

36. Ibid., pp. 72–84.

The final step in Payne's argument was to bring these two considerations together into some type of harmonious synthesis. As it stands, there is an apparent contradiction: the rapture can occur at any time whatsoever, and the rapture will of necessity follow the great tribulation.

Payne tried, in fact, to synthesize the major strengths of the three methods of prophetic interpretation: historical, futurist, and preterist. Some prophecies are of events that have occurred within the church's history between their prediction and the present. Some are of events that will not occur until the very last times. Others are of events that occurred contemporaneously with the prophecies themselves.[37] Payne divided the predicted antecedents to Christ's coming into two classes: potentially present antecedents and future antecedents.

Included in the former class are certain long-range prophecies. One is that the gospel of the kingdom will be preached in the whole world before the end will come (Matt. 24:14). This does not affirm that all will believe or even that all will be evangelized, but simply that an adequate testimony will be preached to all of the world's nations. World missions has been working at this goal and may well have achieved it.[38] Other such prophecies are a divided empire (Rev. 17:12, 14, 16), false security (Matt. 24:38–39), apostasy (II Thess. 2:2–3), lawlessness (II Thess. 2:6–8), and Palestinian Judaism (Zech. 12:10).

Probably the most significant of Payne's potentially present antecedents, for our purposes at least, is the great tribulation. Pretribulationists have tended to make the tribulation totally a future event. Payne argued that Daniel's seventieth week (9:24–27) and the event known as the "abomination of desolation" (Matt. 24:4–22) have preterist significance only. They extend in application no further than A.D. 70. Other prophecies, however, cannot so easily be dismissed as already past. Particularly where there are references to the Antichrist (as in Dan. 7:20–25; 11:40–45; and II Thess. 2:3–11), we may assume that we are dealing with the great tribulation.[39]

---

37. Ibid., pp. 105–6.
38. Ibid., pp. 107–8.
39. Ibid., pp. 113–18.

Payne observed that Scripture does not specify the length of the great tribulation. Any apparent references to its length are quite symbolic in nature and therefore allow several possible interpretations. Thus, the great tribulation may not be very long.[40] While Americans tend to see the tribulation as necessarily distant, Christians behind the Iron Curtain may see it very differently. The existence of powerful political organizations that are opposed to religion and particularly to Christianity, and that are headed by a powerful leader, satisfies the qualifications of the Antichrist. At the time of Payne's writing, Russia and Nikita Khrushchev fulfilled the description beautifully. We may, without realizing it, be in the great tribulation, or at least in one of its early stages.[41]

There are also a few future antecedents of Christ's coming, or of the rapture. These, such as the trump of God, or the wrath of God, are of such brief duration that they will only slightly delay Christ's appearance. They do not negate or dilute the concept of imminence.[42]

Payne's view may be summarized briefly: The pretribulational view that separates the second coming into two distinguishable stages is not defensible. There is only a unitary second coming, and it will follow the tribulation. Christ's coming is also imminent. The supposed antecedents of this event, which could be regarded as presenting an obstacle to imminency, either took place at the time of the prophecy, or are potentially occurring currently, or will be so brief in duration as to pose no serious obstacle after all.

By way of evaluation, we must note the novelty and inventiveness of this view. Payne has made a genuinely creative attempt to break the impasse and bridge the gap between pretribulationism and posttribulationism. The quality of his exegesis is also very good; Payne is at his best when exposing the pretribulationists' unwarranted inferences and arbitrary distinctions.

The weakness of Payne's position is his argument for imminency. He cited the commands to watch, wait, work, and be ready, as well as the statements that the time of the Lord's coming is unknown. He recognized that at the time these passages were

---

40. Ibid., pp. 118–19.
41. Ibid., pp. 119–21.
42. Ibid., pp. 133–45.

written, they could not have meant imminency to the immediate hearers and readers, for some events (such as the fall of Jerusalem) had to occur before the Lord could return. But, said Payne, those events have now occurred and nothing prevents those passages from teaching imminence. This argument, however, seems flawed. If the words of those injunctions did not require the first audience to hold to the doctrine of imminency, then these words obviously contain no inherent meaning that requires imminency. If this is the case, then elapsed time cannot impart to the words a meaning they do not otherwise have. Such would be the case only if Jesus had specified that the disciples were to watch only after these other events had occurred; for example, "Watch, after the fall of Jerusalem." Would it not be better to admit that Jesus did not say that He might come at any moment, but only that the time of His coming is uncertain?

Another way of stating this criticism is this: it is one thing to say we do not know when an event will occur; it is another thing to say that we know of no times when it will not occur. If on a time scale we have points 1 to 1,000, we may know that Christ will not come at points 46 and 79, but not know at just what point He will come. The instructions about watchfulness do not mean that Christ may come at any time. If at the time of the writing, some antecedents had to take place before Christ could come, some other definite signs may still have to be fulfilled. We are to be watchful to help guarantee that these signs will not slip by unheeded.

Conclusion

We have come to the end of our perusal of these several views. We have noted the positions proposed and the arguments advanced by their devotees. I have attempted to treat the various options as fairly and impartially as possible, pointing out both positive and negative aspects of each. Nonetheless, I do hold definite convictions on these issues. Overall, posttribulational premillennialism seems to me the most adequate position. The exegetical arguments for a premillennial coming, particularly those based on Revelation 20, seem to me persuasive. At the same time, the Biblical testimony seems clearly to favor the interpretation that the church will be on earth during the tribulation but will be sustained by the gracious protection and provision of God.

It is important to remind ourselves of the true meaning and purpose of the doctrine of the Lord's second coming. Differences of interpretation and conviction have sometimes become the basis for separation of fellowship. Disputes, sometimes acrimonious, have resulted from these differences. A minute point of doctrine may become regarded as a requisite of orthodoxy and hence of fellowship.

The apostle Paul did not intend the doctrine of the second coming to have such an effect. In I Thessalonians 4:13–18 he indicated that the Lord's coming is the basis of hope for believers and that they are to comfort one another with this hope. Comfort, not contention, is the purpose of this message. Let us recognize as true believers, ones with whom we can have fellowship, all who accept the basic truths concerning the Lord's return, as described in the introduction. As important as it is to understand the points of difference, we must not lose sight of the great basic truth on which we all agree: the Lord is returning. We must make this central. We would do well to heed the often repeated words of the pseudonymous Rupertus Meldenius:

> In essentials unity,
> in doubtful matters liberty,
> in all things charity.

Bibliography

Bass, Clarence B. *Backgrounds to Dispensationalism: Its Historical Genesis and Ecclesiastical Implications.* 1960. Reprint. Grand Rapids: Baker, 1977.

Beasley-Murray, G. R. "The Revelation." In *The New Bible Commentary: Revised,* edited by Donald Guthrie and J. A. Motyer, pp. 1279–1310. Grand Rapids: Eerdmans, 1970.

Beckwith, Clarence. "Millennium." In *The New Schaff-Herzog Encyclopedia of Religious Knowledge,* edited by Samuel Macauley Jackson, 12 vols., 7:374–78. 1908–1912. Reprint. Grand Rapids: Baker, 1951.

Berkhof, Louis. *The Kingdom of God: The Development of the Idea of the Kingdom, Especially Since the Eighteenth Century.* Grand Rapids: Eerdmans, 1951.

Bietenhard, Hans. "The Millennial Hope in the Early Church." *Scottish Journal of Theology* 6 (1953): 12–30.

Boettner, Loraine. "Christian Hope and a Millennium." *Christianity Today,* 29 September 1958, pp. 13–14.

_____. *The Millennium.* Philadelphia: Presbyterian and Reformed, 1957.

Brown, W. Adams. "Millennium." In *A Dictionary of the Bible,* edited by James Hastings, 4 vols., 3:370–73. New York: Scribner's, 1908–1909.

Bultmann, Rudolf. *Jesus Christ and Mythology.* New York: Scribner's, 1958.

185

_____ . "New Testament and Mythology." In *Kerygma and Myth: A Theological Debate,* edited by Hans W. Bartsch and translated by Reginald H. Fuller, pp. 1–44. 1953. Reprint. New York: Harper and Row, 1961.

_____ . *"Zur Eschatologischen Verkündigung Jesu."* Theologische Literaturzeitung 72 (1947): 271–74.

Buswell, James O., Jr. *A Systematic Theology of the Christian Religion.* 2 vols. Grand Rapids: Zondervan, 1962–1963.

Cave, William. *The Lives of the Apostles, and the Two Evangelists Saint Mark and Saint Luke.* Rev. ed. Oxford: Vincent-Tegg, 1840.

David, Ira E. "Translation: When Does It Occur?" *The Dawn* 12 (1935): 358–60.

Dodd, Charles H. *The Apostolic Preaching and Its Development.* Chicago: Willett and Clark, 1937.

_____ . *Gospel and Law: The Relation of Faith and Ethics in Early Christianity.* New York: Columbia University, 1951.

English, E. Schuyler. *Re-Thinking the Rapture: An Examination of What the Scriptures Teach as to the Time of the Translation of the Church in Relation to the Tribulation.* Travelers Rest, S.C.: Southern Bible, 1954.

Fairbairn, Patrick. *The Typology of Scripture, Viewed in Connection with the Whole Series of the Divine Dispensations.* 2 vols. 1900. Reprint (2 vols. in 1). Grand Rapids: Baker, 1975.

Feinberg, Charles L. *Premillennialism or Amillennialism? The Premillennial and Amillennial Systems of Interpretation Analyzed and Compared.* Grand Rapids: Zondervan, 1936.

Fosdick, Harry Emerson. *The Modern Use of the Bible.* New York: Macmillan, 1924.

Gaebelein, A. C. *"Hath God Cast Away His People?"* New York: Gospel, 1905.

Govett, Robert G. "One Taken and One Left." *The Dawn* 12 (1936): 515–18.

_____ . *The Saints' Rapture to the Presence of the Lord Jesus.* London: Nisbet, 1852.

Grier, W. J. "Christian Hope and the Millennium." *Christianity Today,* 13 October 1958, pp. 18–19.

Gundry, Robert H. *The Church and the Tribulation.* Grand Rapids: Zondervan, 1973.

Haldeman, I. M. *The Coming of Christ Both Pre-Millennial and Imminent.* New York: Cook, 1906.

───────── . *The Kingdom of God.* New York: Fitch, 1931.

Hamilton, Floyd E. *The Basis of Millennial Faith.* Grand Rapids: Eerdmans, 1942.

Harnack, Adolf von. "Millennium." In *Encyclopaedia Britannica,* 9th ed., 16:314–18. New York: Scribner's, 1883.

───────── . *What Is Christianity?* Translated by Thomas Bailey Saunders. 3rd ed. 1904. Reprint. New York: Harper, 1957.

Harrison, Norman B. *The End: Re-Thinking the Revelation.* Minneapolis: Harrison, 1941.

Hodge, Charles. *Systematic Theology.* 3 vols. 1871–1873. Reprint. Grand Rapids: Eerdmans, 1946.

Hughes, James A. "Revelation 20:4–6 and the Question of the Millennium." *Westminster Theological Journal* 35 (1973): 281–302.

Kevan, Ernest F. "Millennium." In *Baker's Dictionary of Theology,* edited by Everett F. Harrison, pp. 351–55. Grand Rapids: Baker, 1960.

Kromminga, Diedrich H. *The Millennium in the Church: Studies in the History of Christian Chiliasm.* Grand Rapids: Eerdmans, 1945.

Ladd, George E. *The Blessed Hope.* Grand Rapids: Eerdmans, 1956.

───────── . *Crucial Questions About the Kingdom of God.* Grand Rapids: Eerdmans, 1952.

───────── . "Israel and the Church." *Evangelical Quarterly* 36 (1964): 206–13.

───────── . "Kingdom of God—Reign or Realm?" *Journal of Biblical Literature* 81 (1962): 230–38.

───────── . "The Revelation of Christ's Glory." *Christianity Today,* 1 September 1958, pp. 13–14.

───────── . "Revelation 20 and the Millennium." *Review and Expositor* 57 (1960): 167–75.

Lang, George H. *The Revelation of Jesus Christ: Select Studies.* London: Oliphants, 1945.

Lewis, Gordon. "Biblical Evidence for Pretribulationism." *Bibliotheca Sacra* 125 (1968): 216–26.

_____ . "Theological Antecedents of Pretribulationism." *Bibliotheca Sacra* 125 (1968): 129–38.

MacCulloch, J. A. "Eschatology." In *Encyclopaedia of Religion and Ethics,* edited by James Hastings, 12 vols., 5:373–91. New York: Scribner's, 1913–1922.

Meeks, M. Douglas. *Origins of the Theology of Hope.* Philadelphia: Fortress, 1974.

Moltmann, Jürgen. "The Crucified God." *Interpretation* 26 (1972): 278–99.

_____ . "Hope and History." *Theology Today* 25 (1972): 369–86.

_____ . "Politics and the Practice of Hope." *Christian Century,* 11 March 1970, pp. 288–91.

_____ . "Theology as Eschatology." In *The Future of Hope: Theology as Eschatology,* edited by Frederick Herzog, pp. 1–50. New York: Herder and Herder, 1970.

Payne, J. Barton. *The Imminent Appearing of Jesus Christ.* Grand Rapids: Eerdmans, 1962.

Poiret, Pierre. *The Divine Oeconomy; or, An Universal System of the Works and Purposes of God Towards Men, Demonstrated.* 6 vols. London, 1713.

Ritschl, Albrecht. *The Christian Doctrine of Justification and Reconciliation: The Positive Development of the Doctrine.* Edited and translated by H. R. Mackintosh and A. B. Macaulay. Edinburgh: Clark, 1900.

Robertson, A. T. *A Grammar of the Greek New Testament in the Light of Historical Research.* 4th ed. Nashville: Broadman, 1934.

Ryrie, Charles C. *Dispensationalism Today.* Chicago: Moody, 1965.

Schweitzer, Albert. *The Mystery of the Kingdom of God: The Secret of Jesus' Messiahship and Passion.* Translated by Walter Lowrie. London: Black, 1914.

_____ . *The Quest of the Historical Jesus: A Critical Study of Its Progress from Reimarus to Wrede.* Translated by William Montgomery. 3rd ed. London: Black, 1954.

Snowden, James H. *The Coming of the Lord: Will It Be Premillennial?* New York: Macmillan, 1919.

Summers, Ray. *The Life Beyond.* Nashville: Broadman, 1959.

_____ . "Revelation 20: An Interpretation." *Review and Expositor* 17 (1960): 176–83.

_____ . *Worthy Is the Lamb: An Interpretation of Revelation.* Nashville: Broadman, 1951.

Tyrrell, George. *Christianity at the Cross-Roads.* New York: Longmans and Green, 1910.

Visser, A. J. "A Bird's-Eye View of Ancient Christian Eschatology." *Numen* 14 (1967): 4–22.

Walvoord, John F. "Dispensational Premillennialism." *Christianity Today,* 15 September 1958, pp. 11–13.

_____ . "Israel's Restoration." *Bibliotheca Sacra* 102 (1945): 405–16.

_____ . *The Millennial Kingdom.* Findlay, Ohio: Dunham, 1959.

_____ . "Premillennialism and the Tribulation." *Bibliotheca Sacra* 113 (1956): 1–15.

_____ . *The Rapture Question.* Findlay, Ohio: Dunham, 1957.

_____ . *The Return of the Lord.* Findlay, Ohio: Dunham, 1955.

_____ . *The Thessalonian Epistles.* Findlay, Ohio: Dunham, 1955.

Warfield, Benjamin B. "The Millennium and the Apocalypse." In *Biblical Doctrines,* pp. 643–64. New York: Oxford University, 1929.

Weiss, Johannes. *Jesus' Proclamation of the Kingdom of God.* Edited and translated by Richard H. Hiers and David L. Holland. Philadelphia: Fortress, 1971.

General Index

191

Scripture Index